OBERAM...

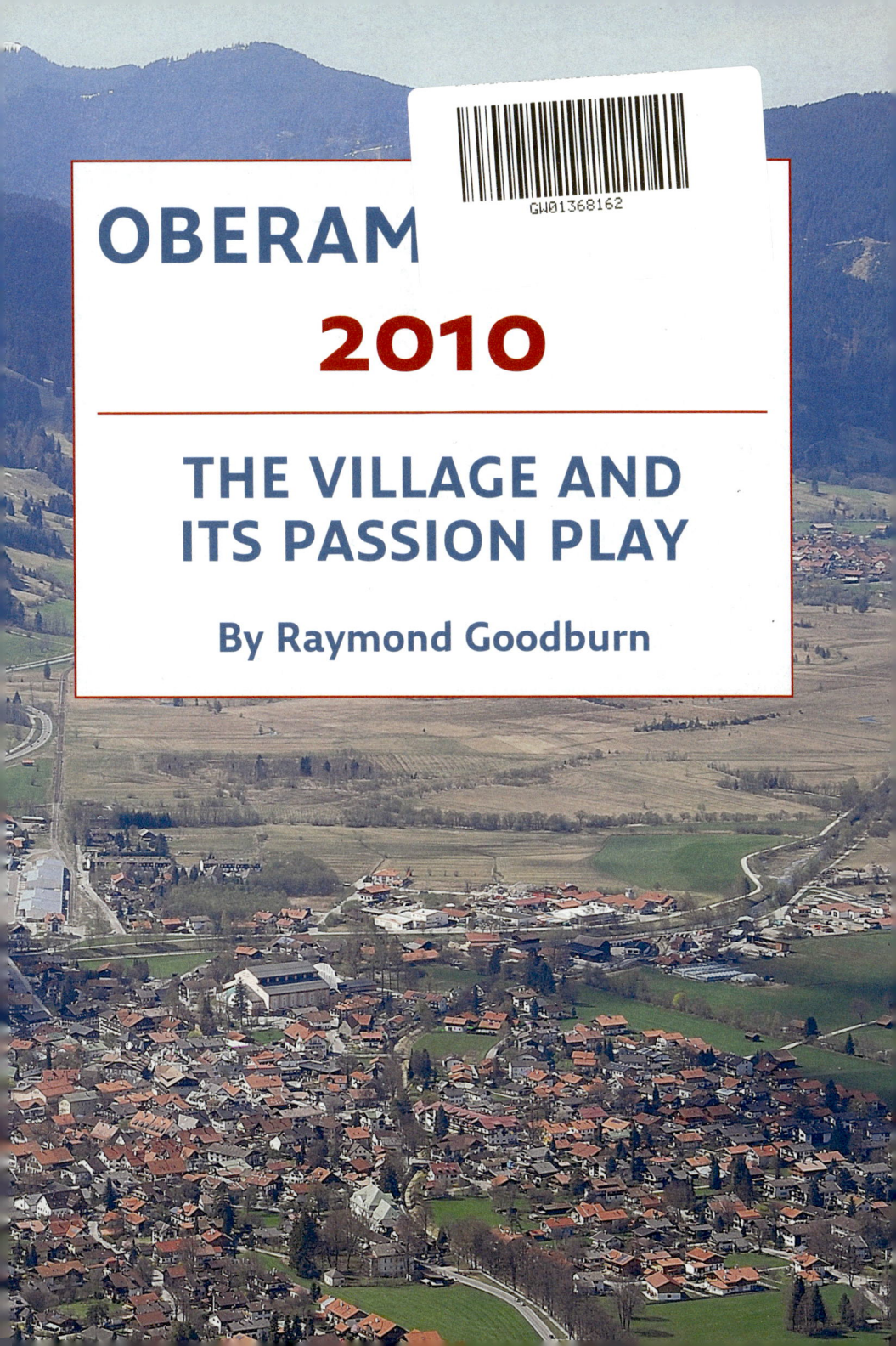

2010

THE VILLAGE AND ITS PASSION PLAY

By Raymond Goodburn

CONTENTS

Welcome to Oberammergau – by Otto Huber	4
The Setting and the Story	7
A Tour of the Village	11
An Introduction to the Passion Play	17
The Play – Organisation and Traditions	25
A Map of the Village	32
The Passion Play Theatre	34
Visits in the Surrounding Area	38
People and the Play	42
Selecting the Cast	47
Practical Information	51
Following the Action – a Synopsis of the Play	53

The author and Publishers wish to acknowledge the considerable assistance given in the preparation of this book by the staff of Oberammergau und DER Reisebüro oHG Geschäftsstelle der Passionsspiele 2010, and in particular Frederik Mayet. Members of The Passion Play Committee, including Otto Huber, Christian Stückl and Markus Zwink. Pictures from the Oberammergau Passion Play 2000 are reproduced with permission of Oberammergau Tourismus. Pictures of Stefan Hageneier, Martin Norz and the Tableau The Loss of Paradise © Thomas Dashuber / Oberammergau Passion Play 2010.

The Entry into Jerusalem 2000

WELCOME TO OBERAMMERGAU

From Otto Huber, Deputy Director and Dramatic Adviser of the Passion Play

I am delighted to have this opportunity of sending you greetings, and extend a warm welcome to the 2010 Passion Play!

I would like to begin with a personal story. In 1950, as a small child, I entered Jerusalem with Jesus during the Passion Play; in 1960 I stood, a teenager, on the Passion stage where I played the part of Isaac in the living tableau in which he ascended Mount Moriah with his father Abraham in order to be sacrificed – a model for Christ's sacrifice on Golgotha. At that time – as during Passion Plays before and since – numerous guests were staying at my parents' guest house. One of them – a devout bus conductor – came from Ashby de la Zouch in Leicestershire. He invited me to England where I, a country lad, was to learn a little about the wide world. This is just one of many examples of how this play, that has come down to us over the ages, brings together people from all over the world. Perhaps, in these peaceful moments of fraternity during the play in our small village on the northern edge of the Alps, something can be felt of the spirit which the Prince of Peace wished to bring us all as he rode into Jerusalem on his donkey. At any rate, it is Oberammergau's calling to tell His story and thereby pass on something of His spirit.

From the outset, it is important for Oberammergau that there is a spirit of hope and of the strength to live. After all, this play of life and death was the result of a promise made at a moment of mortal danger, and the people of Oberammergau fulfilled this promise for the first time in 1634, on a stage which they built in the cemetery, above the fresh graves of those who had died of the plague.

In 2010 the community of Oberammergau is performing for the 41st time this play that it has carried through the ages in a unique example of continuity. When passion plays were banned in Catholic southern Germany in the 18th century when the spirit of rationalism held sway, Oberammergau alone was able to resume. Was this due to its commitment to the vow? To the conviction reflected in the impressive creative joy of the skilled craft workers? Or was it the literary and theological support from the nearby monasteries of Ettal and Rottenbuch that proved decisive?

But the people of Oberammergau were not content to simply repeat the play – they developed it. This is why there have been different versions of the text, culminating in the revised version produced by Father J.A. Daisenberger, used from 1860 to the present day.

The production concentrated, under the title 'The Great Sacrifice on Golgotha', on the Saviour's suffering and death. However, less was made of his message, which brought him into conflict with the whole world. In 2010, on the other hand, we are attempting to place greater emphasis on his call for a radical change of ideas, his commandment to love God and Man.

All of the drama is there: Jesus spoke to a world without peace that was ruled by Rome and marked by social conflicts, based on suppression and exploitation. People longed for freedom from foreign rule, the burden of taxation and slavery, and for a Messiah who would bring peace and justice.

Jesus proclaimed a new image of Man: God is in everyone, the measure of our love of God is the charity we show to those nearest to us. He broke the chain of hate and counter-hate, force and counter-force. It is this Jesus, who constantly advocates belief in his God, the God of Abraham, Isaac and Jacob, that we wish to show.

So too with the musical living tableaux inserted into the action. These comparative flashbacks to the faith experiences of the Israelites, also help to bring His faith closer in an emotional way. We have done more work on these for 2010, and on the text as a whole, music, sets and costumes.

We hope to reach you with our play and that for you, too, this story will become a source of hope and of the life force.

Tableau – The loss of paradise

The Parish Church

THE SETTING AND THE STORY

Nestling among the Bavarian Alps in the Ammergau Valley is the delightful village of Oberammergau, with a population of about 5,300. The Ammergau Valley has been an important communications route for centuries. Indeed, research suggests traces of settlements in the upper Ammer valley dating back to Celtic times. During the Roman period it lay on the military route from Verona to Augsburg and in common with most of the passable routes across the Alps it has been fought over time and again. Eventually the Ammergau region became the centre of a far-reaching area and from the 9th century onwards it was the religious focal point for the entire valley. Subsequently it was in the hands of many different rulers, but most importantly as part of the lands of the Dukes of Bavaria, culminating with the rule of the 'mad' King Ludwig II, a close friend of Richard Wagner and builder of the nearby 'fairy-tale' castles.

The village stands more than 2,500ft above sea level in a valley almost totally surrounded by mountains. From a southerly and easterly direction it is

Fresco showing the first Play

approached by a road which winds its way up from the autobahn between Munich and Garmisch-Partenkirchen. The other main road takes a northerly direction, following the river Ammer through the 'twin' village of Unterammergau, and then to Schongau and north towards Augsburg.

Coming from the direction of Garmisch the road passes through the village of Ettal, with its huge Monastery and fine church founded in 1330. Oberammergau was administered from here for many years, and the Monastery and its incumbents have always had a great influence on the Passion Play, as we shall see later. Together with its fellow monastic institutions at Rottenbuch and Steingaden, Ettal forms a geographical triangle in the southern corner of which lies Oberammergau.

In its trade route days the people of Oberammergau made a good living from providing transport and lodgings for the traveller. But in the winter it was a very different story. Once the snows arrived, those who lived in the mountains could not move far from their homes and so they developed the art of woodcarving, a skill for which the village is still renowned today. They would spend the winter carving toys, religious figures and household utensils, and when summer came they would set off to peddle their wares in the surrounding area and beyond, carrying their goods on a large wooden frame slung over their back. In the centre of the village there used to be a wooden representation of just such a pedlar, but unfortunately this became so damaged by the ravages of the climate that it had to be taken down. The nearest approximation you can find these days is on the road out of the village in the direction of Ettal where eventually, on the right, you will see a pedlar modelled in stone! But in the winter even he is encased in wood to protect him from the winter frosts and snows.

Of the surrounding mountains two in particular stand out. The Laber, on the eastern edge of Oberammergau, is 5,600ft high and can be ascended from the village by cable-car. On the southern edge of the village is the Kofel (4480ft), a sugar-loaf shaped mountain with a great cross on its peak. This is often used as a symbol of the village and it is on the slopes of the Kofel that many of the traditional festivities of the village take place, such as the torchlight procession celebrating the birthday of King Ludwig II.

But what makes Oberammergau so special? The answer, of course, lies in events in the first part of the 17th century. From 1618-1648 the 'Thirty Years War' engulfed much of Europe. It began as a religious conflict between Protestants and Catholics, for even though the Protestant Reformation had happened a century earlier, the two groups had not yet learned to live amicably together. However it gradually developed into a general war across Europe, for reasons not necessarily related to religion, and in its wake brought widespread famine and disease which spread like wildfire across Europe and devastated large parts of Germany. In 1631, the Protestant army of the Swedish King,

Gustavus Adolphus, had heavily defeated the Catholics at Breitenfeld, and went on to take Wurzburg and Munich. The whole of Bavaria was being ravaged by gangs of marauding soldiers who, being unpaid and underfed, went on orgies of rape and pillage wherever they could, so helping to spread the plague or 'black death', which claimed more than a million lives throughout Saxony and Bavaria alone as towns and villages were devastated.

For quite some time the small village of Oberammergau managed to keep the plague at bay, mainly because of its favourable position, surrounded by mountains and accessible only in the summer months. In addition to this there was a strictly enforced quarantine, with guards severely restricting the

The View from the Laber

movements of people in and out of the village, particularly preventing access to strangers. These measures meant that the villagers were able to stay free of the disease until one night an inhabitant of Oberammergau named Kaspar Schisler, who had been living and working away from home at Eschenlohe, evaded the guards under cover of darkness and crept back into the village to visit his family and to share in the Festival marking the dedication of the church. Unwittingly he brought the plague with him from Eschenlohe, only a few miles away and a community which had already succumbed to the disease, resulting not only in his own death and the deaths of his wife and children, but within months 84 adults in Oberammergau are known to have died.

In those days little enough was known about the cause of such diseases, and out of ignorance it was all too easy to concoct remarkable stories in an attempt to explain them. There were those, for example, who were willing to attribute such a disaster to the hand of God and to believe that it was sent as a punishment. Consequently, it was thought that some form of penitence and expression of faith taken in a collective and public way might avert any further wrath of the Almighty. So it was that in July 1633 the village Council, in a desperate act of faith, summoned those who could to meet in the church and there, before the altar, they made a solemn vow to perform, every tenth year, a Play of the Saviour's suffering and death, if God would deliver them from the disease. From that day, it is recorded, no one else in Oberammergau died from the disease.

The performance of a Passion Play in fulfilment of a vow is not unique, but in Oberammergau it has a remarkable record of survival and continuity, despite wars, military occupations, and even an anti-religious edict during a period of secularisation. It is this persistence which has given the Oberammergau Play its prominence among all other such productions, as well as according it world-wide renown. The first performance was given at Pentecost in 1634 by some sixty or seventy performers, on a stage erected over the graves of the plague victims. From then on it was repeated every ten years until 1674, when it was decided to bring the performance to the beginning of each decade. Only twice did the Play not take place – in 1770 when there was a ban on passion plays, and in 1940 due to World War II. Such is the ongoing determination to honour the original vow.

It is strange to reflect that but for the Thirty Years War and the accompanying plague the Oberammergau Passion Play might well never have happened, and that in subsequent centuries any fame for the village would have been much more limited, centred on the quality of its woodcarving and its association with King Ludwig II. As it is, even today the village lives and breathes the Play, for the Play is Oberammergau and Oberammergau is the Play.

A TOUR OF THE VILLAGE

Those who arrive to see the Passion Play will come as part of a wider tour and at the most will spend two nights in the village, arriving the night before the performance and leaving the morning after. Given the new timings for the Play in 2010, afternoon and evening instead of morning and afternoon, that should allow most of the morning before seeing the Play to discover something of the village and do a little shopping! Hopefully, even this brief acquaintance with Oberammergau might act as a stimulus to return another year and stay for longer.

Oberammergau does in fact make an excellent centre for a holiday at any time of the year, and most years welcomes about 70,000 visitors. Hopefully this chapter and a subsequent one about what can be seen in the surrounding area will confirm its appeal as a holiday location. For walkers there are many paths and trails, clearly signed, whether you want a mountain hike or a gentle stroll through the valleys. In addition there are a number of cycle tracks. The area also has excellent winter sports facilities, and in non-Passion Play years there may well be as many visitors here in the winter as in the summer, though that very much depends on the amount of snow, which these days can be somewhat unpredictable. There are a number of ski-lifts, a chair-lift to the Kolbensattel and the cable car to the Laber mentioned in the first chapter. There are several good ski runs and the area is also popular for cross-country runs into the Graswang valley. One famous run, 'In the footsteps of King Ludwig' is just over 30 miles long and is held each year during the first weekend in February. Then, of course, there are the Olympic standard facilities of Garmisch-Partenkirchen, which is only about 12 miles away.

However brief or long your stay, but irrespective of whether you stay summer or winter, one of the first things to strike you about Oberammergau will be the decorated **Frescoes** on many of the buildings, and these are the main visual attraction of the village. Although this particular technique is quite common throughout Bavaria and in parts of the Austrian Tyrol, it is nowhere quite as unique as it is in Oberammergau and as you walk around the village you will see many buildings with painted façades depicting religious themes, rural scenes or fairy tales. In German these frescoes are known as 'lüftmalerei', or 'air painting'. This technique seems to have originated from the practice of decorating Baroque façades in Italy and Southern Germany. It was only in the

18th century that it became popular in the foothills of the Alps, where wealthy traders and craftsmen displayed something of their prosperity by opulently painted façades. This particular art form is accomplished by applying mineral based water colours to wet, freshly laid plaster. As the colours dry they become fixed and insoluble to water. It is a version of the *trompe l'oeil* effect, which tricks the eye into believing that what is basically a two-dimensional painting is in fact three-dimensional.

One explanation of the name for the technique stems from the need to work quickly in the open air (lüft). However, another possible explanation, and one much favoured in Oberammergau, is that it is taken from the name of a house in the village, 'Zum Lüftl', owned by Franz Joseph Zwink (1748–1792) who was a master of this particular skill and much of his craft can be seen around the village. Some of his finest examples (1784) are on the building known as **Pilate's House**, where from the garden side you can see a representation of Jesus being condemned by Pilate. As you look around the exterior the paintings seem to jump out at you with a remarkable 3-D effect. Note how realistic the spiral staircase looks. While you are here a visit inside is also highly recommended, because here you will have an opportunity,

Pilate's House

normally in the afternoon, to watch various people at work demonstrating their particular crafts and also to ask them questions. In addition there is a shop where you can purchase handicrafts from woodcarving to verre églomisé paintings to pottery, all made by members of the studio.

Before moving on from the lüftmalerei, another building of note is the Hansel and Gretel House, which stands on the edge of the village along Ettaler Strasse, the road out towards Ettal. You will be able to recognise many of the nursery rhyme characters – Puss in Boots, Rumpelstiltskin and many more.

Woodcarving is, of course, a long-established skill and still today there are approximately 50 woodcarvers in the village, considerably less than there used to be. As you stroll around the village you will discover many of the shops and workshops dedicated to this particular skill. The roots of the craft go back to the Middle Ages and there is a manuscript dated 1111 which describes how the monks from Rottenbuch brought 'the Ammergau art of carving small household goods out of wood' to the area of Berchtesgaden. In 1520, a traveller from Florence praised the quality of the Oberammergau carvings and in 1563 the Ammergauer carvers received their own Handicrafts Code from the Abbot of Ettal. Initially most of the carvings were sold locally, but by the 18th century many distribution houses were set up with branches all over Europe. From these houses travelling salesmen took on the responsibility of selling the goods from door to door.

Several carvers have their studios open to view and you can sometimes see them at work, with the possibility of purchasing the results. If you are attending the Play you may well recognise some of them as actors. Whilst the quality of the carving does vary and recognising, too, that some of it may not be to your particular taste, nevertheless nearly all the examples on display will have been hand carved in the village, not machine turned and imported. It follows, therefore, that they will not be cheap. As you wander around the village you will certainly find no shortage of shops displaying and selling goods carved from wood. Also, in Ludwig Lang Strasse, on the road towards the cable car station, there is a well-known state run training college for wood carving which is sometimes open to the public. With an international reputation it occasionally mounts exhibitions of its work.

If time permits a visit to the **Museum** should not be missed. This was built between 1904 and 1906 by the architect Franz Zell from Munich, on the order of Guido Lang (1865–1921), the distributor of wood carved goods. Given the importance of wood carving to the village it is not surprising that much of the Museum's display relates to this art. There are crucifixes, figures of saints, needle cases and paperweights created out of maple or fruit-tree wood, all dating from the mid-18th to the late 19th century and all demonstrate the richness of the woodcarver's craft. Moreover, using mainly spruce but sometimes lime wood, the production of toys displays another characteristic of

Frescoed houses in the village

the area. There are dolls, soldiers, fortresses, wagons and carts, mail coach drivers and travellers, coachmen and riders.

A further tradition, dating back to the 18th century, is the carving of Christmas cribs. Prior to this, such nativity scenes had mainly been made from paper and cloth, but in 1760 the woodcarvers created a nativity for their Parish church and for several decades continued to re-model it, with Ludwig himself being a great admirer. This crib is extremely precious and the highlight of the crib display on the ground floor, which should not be missed.

Along with the various examples of woodcarving, there is also a display of verre églomisé, 'Worlds behind glass', most easily described as 'glass engraved on the back and covered by unfired painting'. This was a style of painting which began to develop during the 18th century in the regions of Murnau and Oberammergau and subsequently became a much cultivated craft. Although the Museum already had a notable exhibition of this art form, in 1955 the local authorities acquired a large part of the important collection of verre églomisé belonging to Johann Krotz, a master brewer from nearby Murnau, who by the end of the 19th century had acquired more than a thousand examples.

If you are interested in visiting the Museum during your stay in Oberammergau, you may find it helpful to know that from time to time, in addition to its regular displays, the Museum also hosts special exhibitions. It is normally open from March to October, Tuesday to Sunday.

The Parish Church is dedicated to the Blessed Virgin Mary and the Apostles Peter and Paul. It was built between 1736 and 1742 and is a fine example of the rococo period with a marvellously ornate interior in white and gold. Previous to this present building there had been other churches in the village – first a simple wooden one, in common with churches in the area, then a Romanesque stone one during the Middle Ages, followed by a Gothic one up until the beginning of the 18th century. As this particular building was by then beginning to show considerable damage, almost to the point of being beyond repair, it was decided to construct a new one. There is, as you would expect, some fine carving as well as ceiling paintings, and all the various elements combine to create a wonderfully light atmosphere. Matthäus Günther, an extremely gifted and much respected rococo painter, and Franz Seraph Zwink from the village, were responsible for many of the frescoes, having been brought in by Joseph Schmuzer, one of the greatest Bavarian rococo architects who already had a considerable reputation as a master builder. Much of the stucco work was carried out by Schmuzer's son, Franz Xavier Schmuzer, but in all probability based on his father's plans. Though they may look as if they are created from marble, all the altars and all the statues are carved from wood. If you are fortunate enough to attend a service you will find the standard of the music matches the quality of the surroundings. Indeed, the choir from the church provides some of the singers for the Chorus in the Passion Play. The fine organ is used for teaching local children and is part of the great emphasis placed on music and drama in local education. Fittingly, all the arts of Oberammergau find expression here. There is also a **Protestant (Lutheran) Church** close to the Passion Play Theatre. This is a more modern style and part of its role in the past has been to offer daily Holy Communion services during the Passion Play season.

In Eugen-Papst Strasse you will find a building which has been provided from the funds of previous plays. This is the **Ammergauer House**, a kind of community centre which includes an outdoor theatre, a concert hall and a restaurant, as well as the local **Tourist Office**. If you would like to see where profits from other plays have been spent, you could pay a visit to the **Wellenberg Recreation Centre**, which is near the cable-car station for the Laber, and is open both summer and winter. This really has to be one of the most beautiful recreation centres anywhere in the Alps, with a marvellous swimming pool complex. Here you will find 3 open-air and 3 indoor pools, 2 water slides, an adventure pool, large sunbathing areas, saunas, solarium, and a restaurant and bar.

The Ammergau valley really is an area of great scenic beauty and since Oberammergau is, as already stated, virtually surrounded by mountains, much of this beauty can be appreciated from below. But if you have the time and inclination then do take to the hills. An after-dinner walk across the river and along King Ludwig Strasse offers a panoramic view and an easy climb to the **'Kreuzigungsgruppe'**, a 40ft high stone monument sculptured in marble and depicting the Crucifixion, with the crucified Jesus accompanied by his mother and his closest disciple, John. This was presented by King Ludwig as an expression of his admiration for the people of Oberammergau following his visit to the Play in 1871. Needless to say this was a special performance after the public performances were finished, and attended only by the King and four companions. The *Crucifixion Group* was inaugurated four years later, on the 15th October 1875, to honour the 50th birthday of Ludwig's mother, Marie. The erection of this was not, however, without human cost for during the process both a master stonemason and a stone-cutter were killed when the specially constructed carriage built to convey the statue of St. John overturned and crushed them. Interestingly enough, it was as a result of the King's visit and by his command that the first photographs of the Play's dramatic scenes and tableaux were taken.

AN INTRODUCTION TO THE PASSION PLAY

THE TEXT
The one used for several decades has been basically that of **Alois Daisenberger**, a former priest of the village, for the 1850 performance. The original text, however, seems likely to have been borrowed from other passion plays then in existence, because the tradition of staging the events of Holy Week is believed to be at least 1,000 years old. Moreover, it is probably fair to say that the Oberammergau Play has its roots in the medieval mystery plays, which were common all over Europe in the Middle Ages. They existed in several countries, including Britain, where the plays at Chester and Coventry are still performed. Plays which told the story of Christ's Passion were a later development and are likely to have grown out of the tradition, as regularly happens today, of reading the accounts of Christ's betrayal, arrest, trial, crucifixion and resurrection as an integral part of the Christian liturgy of Holy Week. From this it was only a small step to dramatise the readings, act out some of the main characters and add music. There is sufficient documentary evidence to support the existence of passion plays in the 13th and 14th centuries, but there are very few examples of actual texts until the 15th and 16th centuries.

As far as we can be sure the earliest identifiable Oberammergau text dates to 1662, consisting of 4902 lines based on a late 15th century play from Augsburg and a 16th century play from Nuremberg. In 1674, scenes were added from the Welheim Passion Play, dated to 1600 and 1615, and this in its turn appears to have had its origins in an earlier 15th/16th century Passion.

While there were some revisions to the text in 1720 and 1740, a completely new script was written for the 1750 performance by **Father Ferdinand Rosner**, a Benedictine monk from nearby Ettal monastery. This is often referred to as the 'Passio Nova' and consisted on some 8,547 lines of verse using the formal language of the sacred Baroque theatre. The emphasis in this version was on the Devil as the inspirer and instigator of the treatment meted out to Jesus. Though it created stirring theatre it was open to the criticism that it strayed too far from the New Testament narrative. In 1770 the Bavarian government banned all passion plays but the persistent protests of the Oberammergauers paid off and the Play was once again allowed in 1780 and 1790. For these performances the text was revised, reduced to 4,809 verses and hell was confined to musical interludes!

Not surprisingly there was concern that the authorities might return to their banning ways, so in an attempt to head off this possibility a completely new text was submitted for 1811 by yet another Benedictine monk from Ettal, **Father Othmar Weis**. Out went the Devil and in came the gospels! The aim was to present a drama of the suffering and death of Jesus which was much more in line with the Gospel accounts. Weis also concentrated on the central idea of atonement, removed the allegorical, mythical and legendary elements, and introduced contemporary theology, prose style and wordy, moralising interpretations of the tableaux, along with references to social conflicts. He did, however, keep one dramatic effect from Rosner and that was the special 'living tableaux', eighteen scenes from the Old Testament marking the journey of Jesus through the last days of his ministry. The music for this was composed by Rochus Dedler, a local teacher and about whom more later in this chapter. In 1815 there was a special performance of the Play at the end of the Napoleonic Wars, when there was further extensive revision of the text by Weis and of the music by Dedler. This was also seen as an opportunity to enlarge the crowd scenes, including the 'Entry into Jerusalem'.

For 1850 there were some amendments to the script by Alois Daisenberger, a pupil of Weis and priest of Oberammergau from 1845, who made further revisions at the government's request. Daisenberger gave preference to the Gospel of John and tried to demonstrate the drama of the Passion. By the use of old texts, by warm-heartedness, vivid language and simple symbols, he aimed to 'popularise' the Play, but in the very best sense of the word. Between them Weis and Daisenberger enabled the Play to emerge from a secular era and once again become the dramatic spiritual force it had been in earlier years. Although there were some subsequent changes over the ensuing decades, whether in the text, the costumes, the staging or the music, the Weis-Daisenberger version was to remain the standard until the major reforms of 2000.

The text, however, was not without its controversial elements. It seemed to present a clear contrast between good and evil, the good being the Christians and the evil the Jews, even though, of course, Jesus, his family and disciples were all Jews. It is highly unlikely that the people of Oberammergau had any intention of producing a Play that was deliberately anti-Semitic. Indeed, anti-Semitism as such did not really come into vogue until the latter part of the 19th century, long after the Daisenberger text. It is much more likely that the text was consistent with the prevailing theology and popular conceptions at the time in which Weis and Daisenberger lived and wrote. After all, however unpalatable it is now, there was a long tradition of calling Jews 'Christ-killers', going back, for example, to St. John Chrysostom in the 4th century, who spoke of the Cross being ridiculed 'where Christ-killers gather'.

Difficult too in the text was the much-repeated 'blood curse' of Matthew 27:25, 'his blood be upon us and our children'. The repetition merely served to enforce the prevailing attitude towards the Jews. Nor was the matter helped by the visit of Adolf Hitler to the Play in 1930, accompanied by his propaganda chief, Joseph Goebbels, though, of course, National Socialism had not yet taken control of Germany. The controversy was further compounded in 1934 when Hitler, as Chancellor of Germany, once again attended the Play for the 300th anniversary performances and gave it his approval, writing some eight years later, 'It is vital that the Passion Play be continued at Oberammergau, for never has the menace of Jewry been so convincingly portrayed as in this presentation of what happened in the times of the Romans. There one sees in Pontius Pilate a Roman racially and intellectually so superior, that he stands out like a firm, clean rock in the middle of the whole muck of Jewry'. Not the best advertisement for the Play – to say the least!

Because of World War II there was no Play in 1940 and performances recommenced in 1950. It was inevitable, after the Nazi treatment of the Jews and

Jesus before Caiaphas

all the horrors of the Holocaust, that the question of anti-Semitism in the Play should again be raised. It was not until 1965, however, and the Second Vatican Council initiated by Pope John XXIII, that there was the incentive to re-examine the whole issue. The Council decreed that Christians should show a new and positive attitude towards the Jews and that the Jews, whether ancient or modern, bore no collective blame or guilt for Christ's death.

Certain attempts were made between 1969 and 1989 to revise the text in ways which would counter the criticisms, but although some of the worst caricatures in the text were removed from the 1970 Play, yet still there were fierce protests from both American Jewish groups and some Christian groups. One Rabbi described the Play as 'a nightmare of anti-Jewishness'. An attempt to deal with the situation was made by certain reformers within Oberammergau who suggested ditching the 19th century Daisenberger text altogether and returning to the older and less passionate Rosner version of 1750. After all, Rosner's allegory-filled verses blamed the Devil rather than the Jews for the Passion of Jesus. Money was raised for a trial production in 1977, which was applauded by the critics, but the villagers, who had the final say about the Play and its text, missed the familiarity of Daisenberger. In the 1978 elections to the village Council the supporters of Daisenberger won the day

The Last Supper

and immediately decided that his text would again be used for the 1980 production. There were, however, some changes in an attempt to soften the anti-Jewishness. For example, in the scene when the crowd was shouting for Barabbas to be released, voices were heard calling for Jesus to be set free and Roman soldiers, too, were portrayed as being vindictive towards him, whereas in the past they had often been presented as standing above the whole furore. But still the 'blood curse' from Matthew's Gospel remained.

Yet change, however slow, was waiting in the wings. Representatives of the American Jewish Committee and the Anti-Defamation League began working with leading Catholic scholars and negotiating with the villagers about changes in the Play emphasising, for example, the Jewishness of Jesus as well as the role played by the Roman authorities in his crucifixion. Though the whole matter of the 'blood curse' had been particularly divisive, it was retained for 1990.

Eventually, the criticisms of Jews and Christians, both Catholic and Protestant, began to bear fruit and for 2000 a completely new production was commissioned. In collaboration with Christian Stückl, the Director, Otto Huber, a retired schoolteacher and the Second Director who had been a leading negotiator in the ongoing dialogue, undertook the responsibility of creating the new text which involved 60% of the original text being re-written. Out went the 'blood curse'; the Jewishness of Jesus and his disciples was strongly emphasised; at the last Supper a Menorah was prominently displayed and the disciples were shown wearing prayer shawls; Jesus offered a blessing in Hebrew; and the prosecutors in the Council were challenged by several of their own number demanding a fair trial for Jesus. While the Preface to the 1990 production argued strongly for the retention of the 'blood curse', the 2000 one declared, 'the Passion Play is in no way meant to find a specific person or group guilty or, even less, to assign collective guilt'. There is even the admission in the same Preface, 'that this Passion Play, too, contributed in various ways to preparing the soil which eventually yielded the terrible harvest of the extermination of the Jews. In addition, and significantly, Christians forgot that Jesus was a Jew, like his mother, like Mary of Magdala or all of the apostles, and like the first Christian community'. To assist with all these changes of text, and in particular the matter of how the Jews should be portrayed, a major innovation was the appointment of a Theological Advisor in the person of Professor Dr Ludwig Mödl, a religious historian at Munich University.

In preparation for 2010, many hours have been spent by the Directors, Christian Stückl and Otto Huber, in further adapting the text so as to both project Jesus' radical message of love to a present-day audience and also to banish any lingering criticisms about anti-Jewishness. To this end both Christian and Jewish advisers have provided invaluable assistance.

THE MUSIC

Though there may be less to be written about the music, it does not mean that the musical score is regarded in Oberammergau as any less sacrosanct than the text itself. Far from it! Composed by **Rochus Dedler** (1779–1822), the music has been an integral part of the Play for 180 years and is likely to remain that way. A production without it is hardly conceivable.

Dedler was born in Oberammergau, the son of a local innkeeper. His musical education began as a chorister at the neighbouring Augustinian monastery of Rottenbuch. It continued in Munich, considered at that time to be the best educational establishment specialising in music. Besides having an excellent bass voice he was regarded as someone with an outstanding musical talent. He returned to Oberammergau in 1802 as a teacher, choirmaster and organist and was to spend the remaining twenty years of his life here, achieving considerable fame, both locally and beyond, as a composer primarily of sacred music. In a comparatively short time he had composed more than one hundred pieces, including some twenty Masses and Requiems, which are still sung in the Parish Church.

Unsurprisingly it is his music for the Passion Play by which he is most fondly remembered in the village even today. Prior to Dedler most of the Play's music consisted of Gregorian chants and vocal arias, and whether he was influenced in his composition by any of this earlier music is unknown. He wrote different versions for the Plays of 1811, 1815 and 1820, each time to new texts by Othmar Weis. It must be remembered that even for the 1820 Play he was still writing for a production in the cemetery, which inevitably restricted the size of both the chorus and the orchestra. Dedler himself conducted, recited the lengthy prologues to the 24 Old Testament scenes and, in addition, sang the bass part. This was a colossal undertaking for one person and led to a breakdown in his health from which he died two years later.

His score for 1820 reflected the stylistic tradition of the liturgical music of Franz Joseph and Michael Haydn and was, of course, designed to be performed by amateur musicians. It contained solo parts for all four voice ranges in the form of recitatives and arias as well as many choral numbers. The music acts as mediator between the 'living pictures' of the Old Testament and the drama of the Passion, helping to convey the spirit of the drama.

The change of venue in 1830 from the cemetery to a site on the northern edge of the village meant an altogether more large-scale production attended by larger audiences. This in turn necessitated bigger musical resources which therefore required considerable re-writing of the original. With changes to the text later in the 19th century, some of which involved cuts, the composition had to be further altered. The constant pressure for change continued into the 20th century and this demanded a re-writing of the score for almost every season of the Passion Play. For the 1950 production Dedler's score was greatly enhanced by **Prof. Eugen Papst**, another Oberammergau-born musician, who was a friend and colleague of Richard Strauss. His thoroughgoing adaptation, which among other things added brilliance to the orchestration, led to 40 years of relative musical calm. There was an unsuccessful attempt in 1977 by some in the village to return to Rosner's text and this expressed a desire for the Play to be reformed from what had traditionally been handed down. All this was to pave the way for the enormous changes in 2000, both in the text and the music.

Although the text changes required a re-consideration of the music, the original score of Dedler still lay at the heart of the 2000 production from beginning to end. However, the newly written texts and the new tableaux from the Old Testament needed new music to be composed. This was the enormous responsibility of Markus Zwink, the Musical Director who, to achieve what was required, himself composed new music, but in a style that was in harmony with Dedler, and in addition he adapted and revised some of Dedler's own previously unused compositions. Given that there are further changes to the text and tableaux for 2010, additional music has also been composed.

THE TABLEAUX VIVANTS AND STAGE SETS
The *tableaux vivants* or 'living' tableaux are static scenes, motionless pictures, depicting stories from the Old Testament which are staged between acts of the living Play. For example, the mocking of Jesus is preceded by the tableau of Job

Tableau – Job is comforted

in misery before his so-called 'comforters', and the scene of Jesus on the way to the Cross is prefaced by the tableau of Abraham demonstrating his complete trust in God as he prepares to sacrifice his only son, Isaac. They serve both to hold the attention while the scenery is being changed, as there are no curtains to be drawn, and also to provide a parallel link with the New Testament narrative. They are accompanied by music and usually by the chorus or soloists. The actors in the tableaux are entirely motionless, giving the impression of a living scene frozen in time.

These tableaux have been an integral part of the Play since the 18th century when they were introduced as an aid to prayerful meditation, for at that time they were intended to be seen in silence. They are meant also to reveal a basic truth of human experience and divine revelation, and it is through them that successive Directors have been able to express their individuality.

From 1930 to 1990 the stage sets were those designed by **Johann Lang**, who produced the Play from 1930 to 1960. Though Christian Stückl was appointed Director for the 1990 Play, at that point he really had to work with Lang's sets, but in 1997, having been commissioned by the village Council to prepare a new production, he was able to bring in Stefan Hageneier to design the sets and costumes. In spite of all the changes to sets, tableaux and costumes in 2000, there will be more changes for 2010. The central area of the stage will have a blue back-drop; the previously bare side walls will be adorned with olive trees; the tableaux will be even more colourful, so adding to the dramatic impact of providing a bridge between Judaism and Christianity; and there will be new costumes, all created by 20 women from the village. These changes, all designed again by Stefan Hageneier, plus those to the text, are all part of the Director's determination to keep the Play alive. He is convinced that each production requires a totally new approach.

THE CHRONOLOGY

Much has been said in this and other chapters about the changes that have taken place in the Play over decades and, indeed, centuries. Yet however much it has changed, the outline of the Play has remained the same since 1634. Beginning with the Entry into Jerusalem, it takes us through the momentous events of Holy Week – the Last Supper, Gethsemane, the betrayal and arrest, the mocking and scourging, all leading to the final climactic scenes of the Crucifixion, Resurrection and Exaltation. However much the presentation inevitably changes, the events remain the same and so, too, does the message of the Passion, even though periodically, as in 2000 and again in 2010, it has to be re-presented so as to bring that message home to a contemporary audience.

THE PLAY – ORGANISATION AND TRADITIONS

The **organisation** of the Play is no mean feat, either in terms of the production itself or the managing of some 500,000 visitors from 40 different countries during the season. In fact, the overseas visitors make up some 55% of the total number attending the Play. With a population of 5,300 people there are about 2,500 who are involved in the production in one way or another, either on stage or behind it, in the orchestra or chorus, or dealing with scenery, costumes and 'props'.

Jesus Drives the Traders from the Temple

Since the rest of the population is largely involved in the business of catering for the 4,700 people, plus coach drivers, tour escorts and other staff, who arrive for each performance, coming and going four times a week, it is easy to imagine the colossal impact which the Play makes on the community. Then there is the fact that it also creates some problems in carrying on with every day life, jobs and careers, especially when this disruption happens for only one year in ten. There is only a minute permanent staff retained for the interim years, though the business of tourism does provide many jobs all year round, but for most it is a matter of 'business as usual', not only in the years when there is no Play, but also during the Play season itself. For example, one of the leading actors in the 1990 Play described how he had used up all his annual leave and then had to take extra, unpaid time off, in order to fulfil his role on stage and at the same time keep his employer happy!

As can be imagined, the handling of visitors is a huge operation in itself. In 2010, for three performances a week on Sundays, Tuesdays and Thursdays, tickets will be sold as part of a package which also includes two nights accommodation, with dinner and breakfast, plus lunch on the day of the Play and then departure after breakfast the next morning. Those attending the Play on Fridays will arrive during the Friday morning, have lunch, see the Play with a dinner break included, and then leave after breakfast on the Saturday morning. The Saturday performances are designed mainly for people who live within easy travelling distance of the village, so tickets are sold without the accommodation package. The big difference for 2010 will be that instead of performances being in the morning and afternoon, they will be in the afternoon and evening. More will be said about the reasons for this change later in the chapter.

Because the number of hotels and guest houses is limited, some of the accommodation is provided in private homes. It has long been a tradition in the village for people to open up their houses for visitors to the Play, and for many visitors it is a particular delight to share the home and enjoy the hospitality of a local family. There is strict quality control over the accommodation and food. All rooms are classified and expected to be en-suite, with the Banks making special offers to enable householders to improve the standard of their rooms. Many staying in a private home may well find at least one member of the family is taking part in the Play, even possibly a leading member of the cast. I remember when I first took a group to Oberammergau in 1990 we opted to stay in private homes. In the particular house where some of the group and I were staying, the daughter of the family served our breakfast, said that she would be appearing on stage during the morning and that we should look out for her, but that she would be back in time to serve our lunch! Similarly, during the afternoon she would be on stage yet again, and this announcement also came with the re-assurance that she would be back in the house for dinner, which she most certainly was and keen to know our reaction to the Play. But even with the use of private houses, Oberammergau is still not large enough to accommodate everyone, and some will find that they are staying, whether in hotels, guest houses or private homes, in a nearby village such as Unterammergau or Ettal.

As well as accommodation, there is also the question of transport, as most visitors will be travelling to the village from quite some distance away as part of an organised tour and arriving by coach. In 2000 it was decided that tourist coaches should be kept out of the centre of the village, so there was a system of local shuttle buses to transport visitors to and from the Theatre in those situations where transport was needed and this will be repeated again in 2010. People near the centre of the village can, of course, walk quite easily to the Theatre.

All this coming and going during the Play season gives the impression of a constantly mobile population, for while 5,300 people live and work here, an almost equivalent number are either arriving or departing on 5 days of the week. The only periods of comparative peace and quiet are during the performances themselves, but even then there are constant comings and goings, for many of the cast will have walk-on parts during the bigger scenes and only need to be there for small sections of the Play. In between times they can get on with their normal lives, running their business or homes. Outside the Play season, of course, the village takes on a more tranquil air.

Moreover, the staging of the Play itself requires much organisation. There are a total of 130 speaking parts and two players are cast for each of the 18 main parts, which include Jesus, Mary, John, Judas, Caiaphas and Pilate. Interestingly enough, one of the most coveted roles is that of Judas, who has a major scene and, therefore the stage, all to himself! Previously there were understudies who also took minor roles, but asking any one person to undertake some 100 performances over a period of 5 months is to impose too great a strain, especially if he or she is employed or in business. Also, the selection of two people for the major roles has the advantage of deflecting media attention from the more prominent actors, Jesus and Mary in particular, as considerable effort is made to avoid any aura of stardom being placed on individuals. In the past there have been limited speaking roles for women, but in 2010 a new female character is introduced – Claudia, the wife of Pilate, who appears in person to warn him of her dream. Needless to say there are also a host of smaller parts for players in the crowd scenes or as Roman soldiers. These latter will be more prominent throughout the Play than previously in order to portray the political situation between the Romans and Jews, and part of this will be an emphasis on the relation between Caiaphas and Pilate, to show them in new ways.

With an even larger cast for 2010, some 2400 in total of whom 630 are children, plus a chorus of 48 singers, an orchestra of 55 players, and also the soloists, then the scale of the production can begin to be appreciated. That is without all of the back stage and 'front of house' staff. Indeed, for sheer size of production, let alone anything else, the Oberammergau Play is unequalled anywhere. Nor should the animals be forgotten, the sheep, the doves and, of course, the donkey ridden by Jesus into Jerusalem, as there is much pride in their selection too. In addition, it needs to be remembered that behind the public presentation of the Play is a rigorous schedule of rehearsals which began on 28th November 2009, with at least 3 or 4 rehearsals a week on stage, come rain, snow or whatever!

Not surprisingly, given the Play's long history, it is steeped in **traditions**, though some of them have been gradually eroded over the decades and centuries. To take part, a person must have been born in the village or have lived there for 20 years. At the end of the Second World War there was a considerable influx of refugees from Eastern Europe which expanded the population quite significantly. They were assimilated successfully and became eligible to take part in the Play from 1970. The cast is made up of Catholics and Protestants and some who have no church affiliation, and in 2000, for the first time, a number of the actors came from among the Muslims who live in the village. Any child who attends the local school can also take part, whatever his or her nationality or birthplace, and there are quite a number of service families in the village from the various NATO countries, as that body has a training school nearby. These facts illustrate what the Play is – a production by a village community, when young and old appear together, a 9-month old baby with a 90 year-old veteran.

The production also eschews such modern contrivances as microphones, amplification, wigs or make-up, though for the first time in 2000 lighting was used, but only for the tableaux. Needless to say, the acoustics in the auditorium have to be excellent, and they are. It also means that a large proportion of the male population must grow their beards and hair because traditionally, on Ash Wednesday the year before the Play, the 'Hair Decree' comes into operation. However, some will later have to shave and cut their hair if, for example, they are chosen to play Roman soldiers, who were always clean shaven.

It is the traditions relating to women that have caused the most controversy, especially in recent years. The original position was that no woman could take part who was either married or over the age of 35. However, for the 1990 Play it was decided, though not without much controversy, that married women would no longer be barred, and in fact one of those selected to play Mary was the cause of a headline in a British newspaper, 'Virgin Mary is mother of two'.

At the same time the age limit of 35 was also discarded, the result of sex-discrimination legislation following a case in the state court of Bavaria brought by three women from Oberammergau. Prior to these changes it was not unknown for women to put off marriage for many years in the hope of playing Mary or Mary Magdalene.

Up to and including the 2000 Play, it had been the inviolable tradition that the performances were spread over the morning and afternoon, beginning at 9.30 am and ending around 5.30 pm, with a 3 hour lunch break between the two halves. However, for the 2010 production the Director, Christian Stückl, said that he wanted to spread the performances over the afternoon and evening, beginning at 2.30 pm and ending at 10.30 pm, with a 3-hour dinner break. His main reason for the suggested change was to heighten the drama of the Crucifixion by placing it at night when there could be a more imaginative use of lighting and torchlight. He said that a later performance would 'bring the audience to a different emotional level and improve the quality of the Play'.

The proposal caused considerable division and heated argument within the village. There were those who argued that it would be unwise to have the person playing Jesus, dressed only in a loin-cloth, suspended on the cross in the cold night air for up to half-an-hour, that children would have to be kept up late, that visitors could get lost trying to find the way back to their accommodation, and that the souvenir shops would lose out because visitors would have no time to shop as had previously been the case. Hoteliers complained about the need to provide extra staff late at night to meet the demands of the returning visitors. Others felt it was a much too radical move away from the Play's medieval traditions.

So the scene was set for a battle between the traditionalists and the progressives, though in essence the conflict boiled down to something much more basic, namely, art versus commerce. Consequently, enough signatures were gathered around the village to force a referendum on the issue, and this was held on Sunday, 17th June 2007. As can be imagined the debate was fierce leading right up to the vote, with Stückl declaring that he would resign as Director if the vote went against him. The main street through the village was lined with posters arguing for the night performance and the then Mayor, Rolf Zigon, came out in support of Stückl by declaring, 'highest priority must be given to the quality of the production, rather than how many chambermaids we need'. As it turned out the vote went Stückl's way, with the proposed change gaining a majority of the votes. So a centuries old tradition has been put aside and we must now wait until the end of the 2010 season to assess if the change achieves what it sets out to do.

As the arrangements for 2010 have worked out, commerce should not lose out at the expense of art! It is quite understandable that the shop-keepers of

Karl Führler, woodcarver, will play Simon of Bethany in 2010

the village feared for their livelihoods because clearly the number of visitors during the Play season is crucial to their continued well-being. Initially there seems to have been a concern that visitors would be staying only one night rather than the customary two, but this will not be the case. For three performances a week they will still stay for two nights and with the Play not beginning until 2.30 pm they will have the morning free to discover something of the village and to visit its shops.

The Play is the 'property' of the community of Oberammergau as expressed through its Town Council, and the Council takes all decisions relating to it. It is supplemented in the year prior to each Play by those appointed as Director, Deputy Director and Musical Director, together with the Catholic priest and the local Lutheran pastor, to form the Passion Play Committee. It is the Council that has to put up the considerable capital which is needed to finance each production and it is they who provided the necessary funds for the major refurbishment of the Theatre for 2000. A great deal also has to be spent on the infrastructure needed to cope with the influx of visitors, car parks, toilets, drainage and sewerage systems, all of which have to be upgraded and renewed on a continuous programme of works.

Profits from the Play have always been ploughed back into facilities for the community, residents and visitors alike, for example, the Wellenberg Centre and the Ammergauer House, both described on page 16. The village also boasts a Thermal Clinic for the treatment of rheumatic diseases and a Rehabilitation Centre. Education is very important and especially music and drama, into which a great deal of money is poured. Children are encouraged to take up these arts and those who show talent are given every opportunity to progress, for they are the future of the Passion Play. Indeed, they grow up with the Play as part of their lives. Stefan Burkhart, for example, who played Caiaphas in 2000, first appeared in 1970 when he was only two-and-a-half years old, and Christian Stückl told me that from the age of seven the Play had been very important to him. Whereas in other countries children all have their own special games, whether hide and seek or whatever, in Oberammergau it is not unknown for children to say, 'Let's go play Passion Play', taking on, no doubt, the particular roles which most appeal to them.

There is some reticence when the question of remuneration for the actors is raised. They are, of course, all amateurs and no one is paid a salary as such. But nowadays it is clearly impractical to expect people to give up such a large proportion of their lives to the Play and possibly suffer loss of income in addition. So players are given an allowance towards compensation for loss of earnings. It is clear that no one makes a fortune from it, so it can be assumed that the arrangement is just about right.

KEY

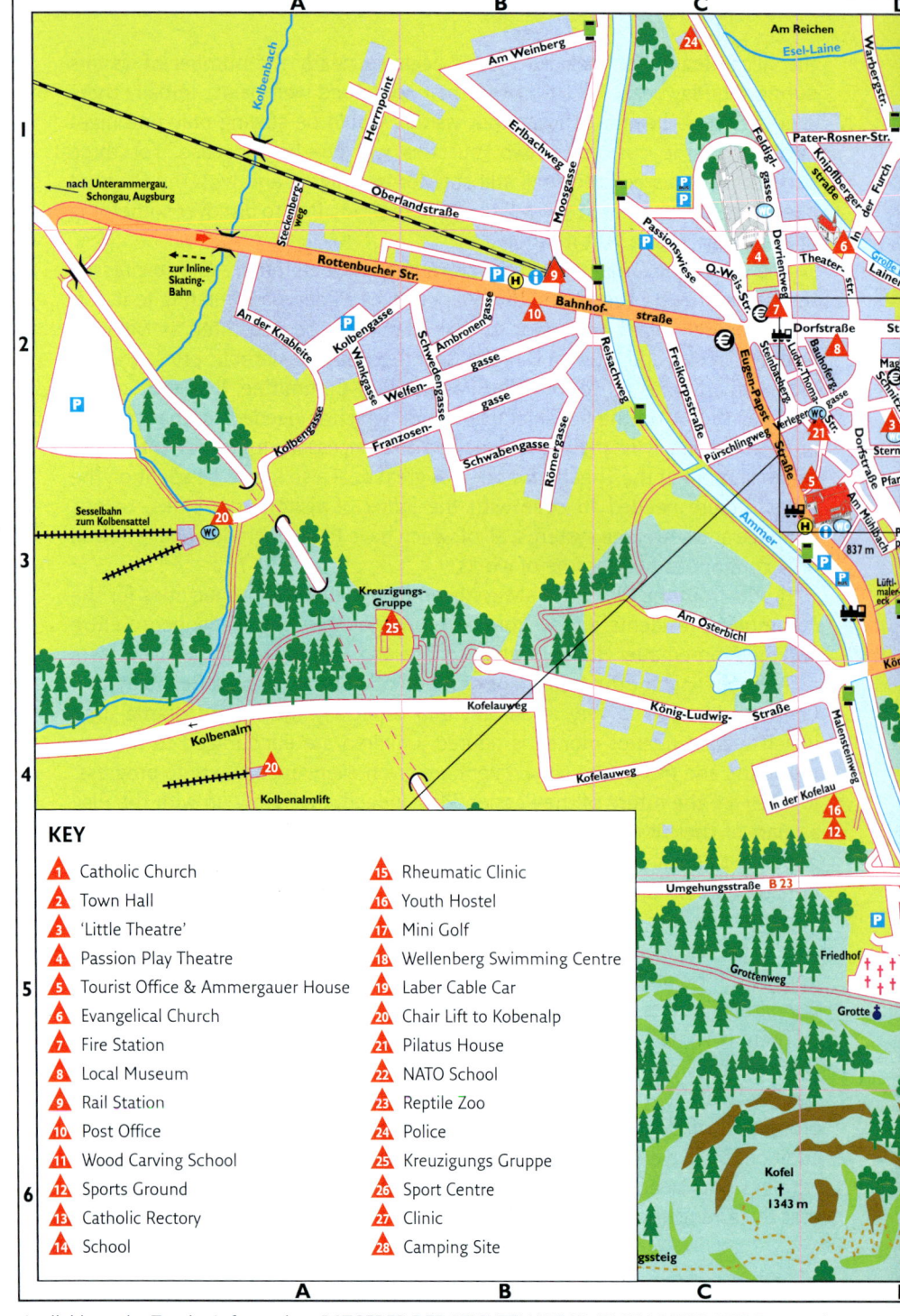

1. Catholic Church
2. Town Hall
3. 'Little Theatre'
4. Passion Play Theatre
5. Tourist Office & Ammergauer House
6. Evangelical Church
7. Fire Station
8. Local Museum
9. Rail Station
10. Post Office
11. Wood Carving School
12. Sports Ground
13. Catholic Rectory
14. School
15. Rheumatic Clinic
16. Youth Hostel
17. Mini Golf
18. Wellenberg Swimming Centre
19. Laber Cable Car
20. Chair Lift to Kobenalp
21. Pilatus House
22. NATO School
23. Reptile Zoo
24. Police
25. Kreuzigungs Gruppe
26. Sport Centre
27. Clinic
28. Camping Site

Available at the Tourist Information: RATGEBER DER LEICHTEN WEGE (EASY ACCESS GUIDE) – getting around berammergau and surroundings in a wheelchair, with a hand bike, rollator or pram (in German)

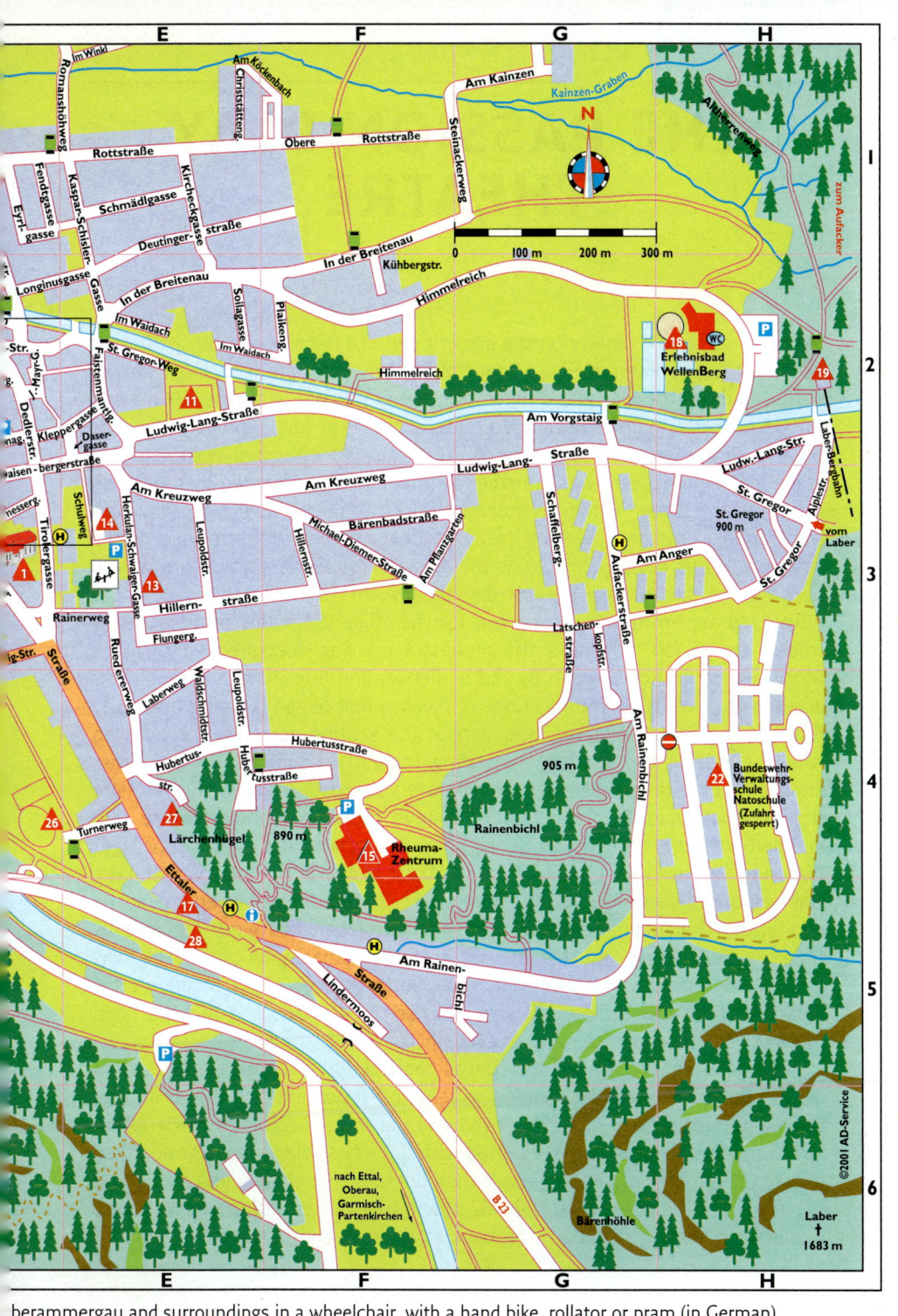

THE PASSION PLAY THEATRE

There has been a theatre on the present site – until more recently dedicated solely to the Passion Play – since 1830. However, the first stage for the performance of the Play was erected over the graves of the plague victims and this is how it remained until 1820. During the 17th and 18th centuries the original simple wooden structure of the stage was equipped with sets and stage mechanics. There was a further overhaul in 1815 designed by the Parish priest at the time, Father Nikolaus Umloch. But in 1830 the Play was transferred from the graveyard to a meadow on the northern edge of the village, and this became known as the 'Passion Meadow'. This in turn was to become the site of the present-day theatre. In 1830 the total audiences numbered approximately 13,000 but for the 1840 series this number nearly trebled to 35,000. For 1880 the orchestra pit was deepened so that the musicians could not be seen by the audience, and interestingly enough this was the year in which Thomas Cook of London first began bringing organised tours to the Play. Ten years later part of the seating area was roofed over, with the rest of the seating area being covered in 1900 by an iron truss structure consisting of six high arches and still existing today. By this time the audiences had risen to 174,000. In 1930 there was a new theatre with an open-air stage, designed by Georg Johann Lang, who also directed the 1930 Play, and Raimund Lang, who later, as Mayor in the post-World War II days, was responsible for reviving the Play in 1950. In the process of enlarging the auditorium the original seats of simple rows of benches were replaced by theatre style seating and this allowed a seating capacity of 5,200. This was the way it remained till after the 1990 performances. As a result of this enlargement, by 1950 the audiences had risen to 480,000 and this has been more or less the constant number ever since.

However, after the 1990 season it was decided that an extensive renovation of both the interior and the façade was required. It was felt that the comfort of the auditorium needed to be improved and the stage mechanics modernised. So in 1997 the villagers were presented with three possible proposals and asked to vote on one of them. Having made their decision, the work began and within two years the theatre was completely transformed. The seating was renewed; under-floor heating installed; the back-stage area and technical equipment modernised; cloakrooms extended; toilet facilities improved; the foyer made accessible for wheel-chair users and exhibition areas added; new fire prevention measures for steel and wooden components were taken, and the exterior was transformed. This new theatre provides 4,720 covered seats, offering the audience maximum comfort and absolute safety. In addition, all these changes opened up the opportunity for more extensive use of the theatre for major cultural events outside the Play season.

No one pretends that the theatre is an architectural masterpiece! It could be likened to a large barn or even an aircraft hangar with its web of iron girders over plain walls. Yet, the rather stark appearance does provide the remarkable acoustical properties which mean that every word spoken on the stage can be heard anywhere in the theatre without any recourse to microphones or loudspeakers. What is more, the design also means that everyone can see as well as hear.

Today's audience is comfortably seated under cover, but in the past the stage has been open to the elements, with the Play continuing whatever the weather conditions could throw at it. But the setting of the stage with its gently rising slopes, the more distant mountains and, hopefully, a few clouds scudding across a clear blue sky, must be one of the most impressively natural for any theatrical performance to be found anywhere. Those occasions when thunder and lightning punctuate the performance may not be comfortable for those on stage, but they can add even more effect to the drama. So it is that the location provides its own scenery and the stage needs to be embellished only by the simplest of effects. The porticos of Pilate's House on the left and the House of the High Priest on the right are the main elements, with the

The Theatre

arches between them representing the entrances to the streets of Jerusalem. The front of the stage becomes the area in front of the Temple, where the main action of the Play takes place.

There is a central stage to the rear, which is covered and has side walls of glass. It is here that the Old Testament tableaux are prepared and presented, as well as some of the scenes of spoken drama. The scene has to be shifted some 40 times during each performance and this requires a considerable amount of technical equipment, including a moveable stage and a drop stage, so that scenes can be prepared below, then hoisted up and rolled forward quickly and almost noiselessly as they are needed, for there are no curtains to be drawn to hide this action as in a normal theatre. There are also electrically driven scene cloths to the central stage, which are wound on to huge steel rollers below.

There is one further significant change to the theatre in addition to those already described for 2000, and that is a retractable roof which has now been built over the stage. Given that in recent years the theatre has been used in non-Play years for a variety of musical and dramatc productions, then clearly an open stage has become increasingly impractical. Christian Stückl, though, is keen to maintain the tradition of an open stage for the Play itself, but no doubt time and climate will tell!

While in previous decades and, indeed, centuries the theatre was reserved exclusively for performances of the Passion Play, it is perhaps hardly surprising that in the 21st century it has been deemed appropriate both artistically and economically to move on from that tradition. Performances since 2000 have included *Elektra* by Richard Strauss, Bizet's *Carmen*, Verdi's *Aida* and *Nabucco*, Mozart's *Magic Flute*, and Bach's *St. Matthew Passion*. During 2008 there were performances of Jeremiah by Stefan Zeig, in which Christian Stückl, Markus Zwink and Stefan Hageneir joined forces (they also collaborated in 2005 for a revival at the theatre of the biblical play King David); Felix Mendelssohn's oratorio, *St. Paul*, conducted by Markus Zwink, when the Ammergauer Motettenchor was joined by choirs from Munich and Innsbruck; as well as performances by world renowned singers and musicians. So, if you ever intend to visit Oberammergau during the non-Play summer months, it might be worth checking to see if there is something being performed at the theatre which might appeal to you.

A further possibility in out-of-season years is to take a guided tour of the theatre and its museum, where you can learn much about the origins and history of the Play, as well as discovering something of its influence on the village and its people. You may also have an opportunity to stand on the huge stage and imagine what it is like for the amateur performers from the village to play their parts in the great drama of the Play. Also back stage you will be able to see the rooms where all the costumes are kept, both the more modern ones and those which are extremely old and valuable, some displaying intricate embroidery. There are other rooms, too, where many items of stage equipment, or 'props', are stored. As can be imagined, some of these are very old – the table and stools used in the Last Supper scene, for instance, date back over 200 years. Such a tour lasts about 45 minutes, and from April to October there are tours in English at 11.00 am and 2.00 pm. There may, of course, be some restriction on these tours when big events are being staged in the theatre.

Before ending this chapter, mention should be made of the fact that as the Play became more known throughout the world from the late 19th century onwards and as travel to Oberammergau became increasingly possible, so the performances over subsequent decades have been attended by a number of famous people. There have been writers like Hans Christian Anderson, Simone de Beauvoir, Thomas Mann, Jean-Paul Sartre and Rabindranath Tagore, composers such as Franz Liszt, Richard Wagner and Anton Bruckner, as well as the engineers Gustav Eiffel and Henry Ford, members of the Russian and Spanish royalty, and not forgetting, of course, Ludwig II himself. Other notable visitors have included Pope Pius XI in 1910, the British Prime Minister, Ramsay MacDonald, in 1930 and Dwight D. Eisenhower in 1950.

The present Pope, Benedict XVI, visited the Passion Play on two occasions, both of these prior to becoming Pope. He first came in 1980 as the Archbishop of the Diocese of Munich and Freising, when he also celebrated the opening worship in the Passion Play Theatre. Then, on the 23rd August 2000, he visited the Play for the second time, on this occasion as Curia Cardinal Joseph Ratzinger, Prefect of the Congregation for the Doctrine of the Faith, at the Vatican.

The Stage

VISITS IN THE SURROUNDING AREA

Clearly how much of the local area you will be able to discover in addition to Oberammergau itself and the Play will depend on the flexibility of your itinerary. Below are some possible options within easy distance of the village.

THE MONASTERY AT ETTAL
In a narrow valley around 3 miles from Oberammergau is the village of Ettal, originally located on an important trade route between Italy and Augsburg. Today it is dominated by the imposing edifice of its Monastery, which was founded in 1330 by an earlier Ludwig who brought back from Italy the white marble Madonna, believed to be a miracle-working statue and which still has pride of place on the altar. Built as a Gothic Monastery it had two abbeys, one for men and the other for women, as well as having a community of knights attached to it, and in due course various residents of the community were to become significantly associated with the Passion Play, particularly in connection with refining and re-writing the text. Nowadays it is still a living Monastery and Parish Church, home to approximately 50 monks.

Though it suffered damage during the Reformation at the hands of the troops of Maurice of Saxony, it did at least survive the troubles of the Thirty Years War. In 1744, the Monastery, its church and a library of 30,000 books were largely destroyed by fire, though the precious Madonna was preserved. Re-built as a splendid example of southern Bavarian Baroque style, the Monastery was later dissolved in 1803 during the time of the secularisation of church property in Bavaria, but was subsequently re-founded as a Benedictine Monastery in 1900. The interior of this impressive church is elaborately decorated in white and gold, a fine example of rococo adornment. The ceiling of the great rotunda is painted with some 400 figures representing St. Benedict and his monastic order, and in the centre of the church hangs a huge chandelier.

The Monastery also has a brewery and a distillery which produces a certain well-known liqueur! In addition there is a bookshop, an art publishing business and even an hotel. A school was founded here in 1709 and this began its educational tradition. These days the school, along with its academic reputation, also boasts a choir greatly renowned in the locality.

The Monastery at Ettal

THE CHURCH AT WIES

Down a lonely country road through forests, some 16 miles from Oberammergau, off the road from Rottenbuch to Steingaden, lies a farm, a meadow, a church and very little else. Standing almost alone, this great church is an important place of pilgrimage for Catholics the world over. It is also one of the richest examples of rococo decoration to be found anywhere in Europe.

Its reputation is built on a legend of the Flagellated Saviour, a statue created by the monks of Steingaden in 1730 to be paraded in the Good Friday procession. However, some years later in 1734 the monks decided that the statue was much too realistic and intense and so was put to one side. Maria Lory, the devout wife of a local farmer, rescued the statue and took it to a farm where it became an object of veneration. Then one day in 1738 she had a vision of the dilapidated statue shedding real tears. When this became public knowledge there was a rush to see it. In 1740 a small chapel was built to house the Flagellated Saviour, but it soon became too small to cope with the large influx of visitors who wanted to venerate the statue. So between 1745 and 1754 the present great church was built, designed by Dominikus Zimmermann, who spent the last 11 years of his life in a nearby dwelling close to his masterpiece. He was assisted in the project by his brother, Johann Baptist. Though the church was secularised at the beginning of the 19th century, protests from local farmers saved this jewel of rococo design and architecture from being demolished.

While the outside is strikingly simple, the inside is strikingly elaborate. Oval in shape the interior is adorned with gilded stucco, wood carvings and vividly coloured frescoes which contrast with the white-washed walls. It has been described as 'exuberant, colourful and joyful'. The quality of the white marble and the gilded decoration, together with the fine carving, impressive paintings and frescoes, all combine to produce a marvellously light effect, aided by the natural lighting through the windows. The church was added to the UNESCO World Heritage List in 1983 and underwent a massive restoration between 1985 and 1991. If at all possible, Wies should not be missed.

GARMISCH-PARTENKIRCHEN

Some 15 miles from Oberammergau, these twin towns, separated by a railway line, have become a by-word for winter sports and as a climatic health spa. Settlers first appeared in the area around 2000 BC and later the Romans established Partanum, which later became Partenkirchen, as a staging post on the military road between Brenner and Augsburg. Originally two towns, each with their own history, they were forced by Hitler to combine in 1935 in readiness for the 1936 Winter Olympics and over the decades since have developed as Germany's best and most famous ski-resort. Traditionally, there is a ski-jumping contest held each New Year's Day and in 2011 the Alpine World Ski Championships are to be held here. The area is dominated by the Zugspitze, at 9724ft the country's highest mountain, and in the summer this can be ascended by mountain railway from the town centre. With mountains all around and Alpine resorts like Lermoos and Seefeld just a short drive away, Garmisch-Partenkirchen makes a good centre for touring the area. It is an attractive town and an excellent shopping centre, with elegant boutiques, art galleries and antique shops. The old part of the town has narrow streets and features wrought-iron signs. This is an especially good place for walkers as there are a variety of lifts and cable-cars quite close to the town. The composer Richard Strauss lived here from 1908 until his death in 1949, and each June he is honoured in the town with a 'Richard Strauss Festival'.

LINDERHOF

Given half an opportunity, do try and visit Linderhof. Only about 8 miles from Oberammergau, it is on the other side of the mountain range which starts with the Kofel, and was inspired by the King Ludwig's visit to Paris in 1867, as a result of which he became smitten with the idea of building a replica, 'a new Versailles'.

Linderhof was the smallest of Ludwig's three castles and the only one he lived to see completed. Though it is much smaller than Versailles it is quite clear that the palace of Louis X1V was its inspiration, with, for example, the staircase at Linderhof being a scaled-down version of the Ambassador's staircase in Versailles. Even the Hall of Mirrors was copied from Versailles. As later with Herrenchiemsee, the overall architect was Georg Dollman, who also employed the talents of other designers.

The castle developed from Ludwig's idea of turning his father's tiny hunting lodge at Linderhof into something grander, though initially it was still intended as a private hunting lodge for the King to enjoy. A miniature masterpiece, building began in 1874 and was completed in 1878. Ludwig regularly stayed here and the royal bedroom has an enormous bed, surrounded by magnificent drapes, golden candelabras and a superb chandelier. One of the reasons that Linderhof is so popular with visitors is because it gives a feeling of being small and intimate, compared with the vastness of Neuschwanstein and the lavish, impersonal character of Herrenchiemsee. There is an atmosphere of domesticity about Linderhof – it looks and feels as if someone could really live here. It became much more like the Trianon at Versailles, Louis XIV's small retreat where he could escape the crowds at the large Palace.

The beautiful terraced gardens cover some 125 acres and combine elements of Baroque style or Italian Renaissance gardens with landscaped sections similar to an English garden. There is a great fountain, lakes and an artificial 'blue grotto', complete with illuminat-ions and a gilded shell-like boat. The great cascade of a waterfall is a splendid sight when it is working in the summer, and in the grounds there is also a Moorish Pavilion which was removed from Oberammergau, where it was found in a dilapidated state, and stylishly renovated. A longer walk will bring you to a Hunting Lodge decorated with scenes from Wagnerian operas. Please note that visits within the castle can only be made with a guided group and these are regularly available in English, lasting about 30 minutes.

Linderhof Castle

PEOPLE AND THE PLAY

Whatever else may be said about the Play, whether in terms of the wording of the text, the styling of the costumes, the performance of the music or the staging of the drama, basically the Play is about people, those who prepare it and those who perform it. In November 2007, in a brief visit to Oberammergau, I was most grateful for the opportunity to meet the Director and Director of Music.

The Director for 2010 will again be **Christian Stückl**, who was first appointed as Director for the 1990 Play when he was only 27 years of age, making him the youngest ever Director. In fact, in 1986 he went to the Mayor and asked if he could direct the Play! Born in the village in 1961, he grew up in the Gasthof Rose, which is today run by his sister, and where he met actors and visitors all talking about the Play. He told me how at that stage he liked to dress up in the costumes and perform lines from the Play, and how he was nicknamed by a former Director as the 'Stage Devil'. This was because he seemed always to be around the Play and its rehearsals, in particular asking questions about the meaning of this sentence and that sentence. Initially he served his apprenticeship as a wood sculptor but having created a group of amateur actors in the village he became assistant director at the prestigious Münchner Kammerspiele in 1987, the same year as he was appointed the Director of the Passion Play. Not unnaturally for 1990, as a younger Director with fresh ideas, he wanted to introduce changes but with little time for manoeuvre and given that Oberammergau changes slowly, he found himself locked into much of the accepted tradition, including the text, though he was able to assign a number of younger actors to leading roles. His style of direction was not without controversy and there were even attempts to dismiss him, but these were narrowly averted. Despite that, however, for 2000 he was commissioned to create a new production, about which much has been said elsewhere.

When asked why, as a professional director, he should want to work with the amateurs of Oberammergau, his response was very affirming. Clearly for him, having grown up with the Play and recognising its importance both for the village and far beyond, there is something very special about working with his own people in his home environment. Interestingly enough, in the 1990 Play, he directed both his father and grand-father who had parts as Judas and Annas respectively, and will be again directing his father in 2010. In talking with him about the way in which he works with the cast one particularly important piece of information came out. Since becoming Director he has done much to encourage younger actors to take on principal roles and so, as part of the preparation for the Play in 1989 and 1999, he went with them to Israel so that they could experience something of the setting and background to the Passion story, and the same happened in 2009. While in the past it has been the local Town Council who have had the responsibility for choosing the cast, increasingly he has hoped that he would be allowed to choose the people he wants for the major roles, and this is how it turned out for 2010 after a four hour meeting.

Since 1990 his career as a professional director has gone from strength to strength. In 1991 he became principal Director of the Münchner Kammerspiele, a post which he held until 1996 when he became a freelance director. He has been a guest Director in cities such as Bonn, Frankfurt, Karlsruhe, Hannover and Vienna. More than once he has directed several of the Shakespeare plays, including 'A Midsummer Night's Dream' in India. Then in 2002 he took up the appointment as manager and artistic Director of the Munich Volkstheater, where he is noted for his radical productions and encouragement of younger talent. In the same year he was Director of 'Everyman' at the Salzburg Festival, followed in 2004 by his first opportunity to direct an opera, Beethoven's 'Fidelio', at the Opera House in Cologne. In the chapter on the Passion Play Theatre, Oberammergau, we have already noted the various productions he has directed there since 2000.

It could be assumed that with all the changes in 2000, there might now be a period of relative stability. Not so! After all, for 2010 there has already been the enormous alteration of the performances being in the afternoon and evening, plus the changes to the text, costumes and tableaux already referred to. When I asked him about any forthcoming changes, his comment was, 'For the Play to live, it must evolve'. On the basis of that there is one thing of which we can be certain, namely, that while he is the Director the Play is unlikely to stand still. And clearly if the Play is both to appeal to future generations and challenge them about the meaning of Christ's death and resurrection, it must do so against the background of a changing world. This in turn means discovering the delicate balancing act of respecting tradition while responding to the present, and I believe that Christian Stückl acknowledges this.

We have already noted the significance of music in the Play and once again in 2010, as for 1990 and 2000, the Musical Director will be **Markus Zwink**. He was born in Oberammergau in 1956, and after the completion of his education at the Ettal Secondary School in 1975 went on to study music at the Mozarteum in Salzburg and the Munich Music Academy. During this time he had the opportunity to be a guest conductor with Nikolaus Harnoncourt. In 1980 he was the bass soloist in the Play and from 1984 to 1997 taught at the Ettal Secondary School, while also being appointed music director of the municipality of Oberammergau in 1985, a post which he has held ever since. In this capacity he runs a number of local choirs, boys, youth and adults, and his wife also runs a girls choir, all this being part of the village tradition of singing and music.

One wet morning in Oberammergau, he provided me with some extremely helpful information about the musical side of the Play. The chorus is chosen from the Ammergauer Motettenchor, of which he is the Founder and Director, and the Choir of the Catholic Church, whose choir master is **Michael Bocklet**, the second conductor for the Play. The chorus and orchestra for any one performance have about 50 singers and players each, and these are drawn from a pool of around 100 singers and a similar number of instrumentalists. Many of those singing in 2010 also sang in 2000, so when it comes to rehearsals most of the chorus will know the words and music, both of which have to be memorised. To sing in the chorus is much sought-after due to its prominent position on the stage, constantly in front of the audience! There is only one point in the Play where the singers are actors in the drama and that is in the great scene of the Entry into Jerusalem. However much he wishes it could be otherwise, tradition makes it very difficult to develop more integration between choir and actors.

Markus Zwink, Music Director

In the same way that more than one actor is assigned to each of the major roles, so it is with the soloists, with 3 or 4 being chosen for each voice. Sometimes even that may not be enough, as there was an occasion in 2000 when all three bass soloists were ill at the same time and Markus Zwink had to take over the bass role. Selection of the choir for 2010 took place in Spring 2009, with the twice-weekly rehearsals beginning in the autumn. The soloists, however, were selected even earlier, in 2008. There is a great deal of interest in solo singing and an early start is made with younger singers in assessing their ability to go further. Those who show promise are required to have ten hours training with professional voice teachers from Munich and then they must audition in front of a professional panel.

In the section on *The Tableaux Vivants* and Stage Sets, something of the crucial work of **Stefan Hageneier** has already been described. Another native of the village and born in 1972, he later became a graduate from the

Oberammergau Wood Carving School, and actually took part in the Play as an extra in 1990, and in 2000 shared the role as Teller of the Prologue with Otto Huber.

But as in 2000, for the next production of the Play his particular talents will mainly be employed behind the scenes, and the many set and costume changes for 2010 have previously been described. These days much of his work is in Munich, collaborating there with Christian Stückl among others, but his skills as a designer have also taken him to New York as well as other major German theatres. He has enjoyed, both before and after 2000, a prominent career both nationally and internationally, working with a variety of eminent directors in Brussels, Zurich, Vienna, Hannover and, of course, Munich.

Stefan Hageneier, Designer

We have already noted the significant contribution of **Otto Huber** in undertaking the huge task of re-drafting the text for 2000 and who, in both 1990 and 2000, also held the responsibility of second Director, as well as being Teller of the Prologue on both occasions. Born in Oberammergau in 1947 he became another product of the Ettal Monastery School and as well as being a teacher he has devoted much of his time to producing drama in the local area. In 2010 he will again have the dual role of second Director and teller of the Prologue. Retired from teaching, he runs the family guesthouse with his wife. These, then, were the people who were the creative team behind the 2000 production, along with Professor Dr Ludwig Mödl, as Theological Adviser, and all of them are sharing that function again next time.

By now it will have become clear that there are certain strong family connections both with Oberammergau and with the Play. A look at some of the names around the village, and in particular in the cemetery of the Catholic Church, is a clear indicator of this. Reference has already been made to Otto Huber, whose family association goes back as far as 1680. His grandfather, Huber Rutz, played Caiaphas three times and Peter in 1950.

Then there is the **Preisinger** family, with Anton Jnr. now running the Alte Post Hotel and having played Judas in 2000. His father played Pilate in 1980 but his grand-father, the late Anton Snr. was one of the most formidable figures of the village from 1950 when he played Jesus and took the same role again in 1960. He then became Director for the 1970 Play and subsequently took smaller parts in both 1980 and 1984, ending in the manner he began when at the age of 10 he was an angel and then Lazarus in 1934.

Theirs, however, is recent history compared with the **Zwinks**, a family who go back at least as far as 1446. Markus, whom we have already met, is a descendant of Frank Seraph Zwink (1748-1792), the gifted rococo painter who created most of the earlier frescoes on the houses in the village. In terms of the Play itself, for example, there were three Zwinks in the 1890 production – Rudolf (Jesus), Ottilie (Mary) and Johann (Judas).

Another well-known name is that of **Lang**. They have one of the proudest of family records up to the time of Walter Lang, who played Nicodemus in 1990. The family of Josef Lang settled in Oberammergau in 1736 and it was they who later, in 1886, set up the state wood-carving school. A Lang has played the part of Christ no less than 5 times – Anton in 1900, 1910 and 1922, who depicted the more gentle side of Jesus, and Alois in 1930 and 1934, who concentrated more on his heroic nature. However, they lost their 'claim' to the role in 1950 when Anton Preisinger was chosen as Christ, after much local disagreement about who should perform the part.

While much has already been said about Christian Stückl, the Director, in various parts of the book, it is important to acknowledge the **Stückl** family association through his father, Peter, and grandfather, Benedikt, both of whom were in the 1990 production when Christian first became Director. In that year Peter played Judas, having previously been Caiaphas in 1980 and 1984, and Benedikt was Annas, the High Priest, a role which he again under-took in 2000 at the age of 76. He first took part in 1930 and in 1980 was Caiaphas and Herod in 1984. It is worthy of note that the name of Stückl and that of Zwink were among the original signatories to the vow in 1633.

Before leaving this chapter it is only appropriate to indicate that not everyone who takes part in the Play is a person of profound religious commitment. Far from it! For some it is seen as part of the village's tradition and culture, something regarded by them and the community as uniquely significant and, therefore, as something in which they wish to be involved.

Christian Stückl, Director

SELECTING THE CAST

There's a sense in which the Play began on the 8th April 2009. How come? Because that was the day in which the village both solemnly renewed the original vow and publicly announced the cast for 2010. Previously these two significant events had been conducted on two separate occasions, but in 2009 it was decided to combine them and what a remarkable and, indeed, moving day it was.

We began at 09.30 in the Parish Church, standing room only, for a short act of worship with hymns, readings and prayers. Then following the town band we processed through the village, paused at the Lutheran Church for further prayers, before moving on to the Theatre itself where, on the stage, the Passion Play orchestra and choir were already seated, along with the town band, and Bavarian television crews were making their final preparations to broadcast live the solemn renewal of the original vow made in 1633.

The occasion took the form of an ecumenical service conducted by the Catholic auxiliary bishop, the priest of the Parish Church, the Lutheran pastor and the Lutheran regional bishop. During this some of the Passion music of Rochus Dedler was played and sung by the choir, and Christoph Stöger, an 11-year old altar boy from the Parish Church, made the renewal of the vow on behalf of the village, to which the villagers in the Theatre responded. Christian Stückl then brought on to the stage all the children who sing as part of the great opening scene of Palm Sunday, when in the Play itself they, the choir and all who are on stage greet the entry of Jesus into Jerusalem by singing the wonderful chorus, 'Hail to you, O David's Son'. But on this Renewal day it was the audience who had the opportunity to sing with them, along with the choir and orchestra. It was a very moving finale.

After a break for lunch came the announcement of the cast, and outside the Theatre there was a great sense of excitement and anticipation among the several hundred people as to who would have the major roles. Prior to the election of the cast more than 1800 adults and 600 children from the village had filled in forms so that their names could go forward to be part of the next Play. Some male villagers specifically asked to be Roman soldiers as this meant that they could shave and cut their hair! The previous evening the Council met for

Jesus will be played by Frederik Mayet (left) and Andreas Richter

four hours in closed session to debate the recommendations of the Director and eventually, not without some heated discussion and controversy, his requests were met. So the time came to declare the names. Who would be Jesus? Painstakingly the name begins to be written on the board – Frederik. But which Frederik? After all, it is a common enough name in these parts. Then the surname is written up.......Mayet. This was very much a surprise choice, possibly even controversial, but he and Andreas Richter will take the role of Jesus. The Director had gone for young talent, which increasingly has been his intention. Each of these young actors will be given the freedom to interpret Jesus in his own way, obviously under the guidance of the Director, and by the time of the first performance on 15th May 2010 both young men will have grown into their role and take their place in a distinguished line of Oberammergau Jesus's of the past.

Mary is played by Ursula Burkhart and Andrea Hecht

And what about Mary? This role will be shared by Ursula Burkhart and Andrea Hecht, both in their late 40s and both of whom have played this role on a previous occasion. Then two very excited young ladies, both in their twenties, Barbara Dobner and Eva-Maria Reiser, will undertake their first principal parts by sharing the role of Mary Magdalene. So the process continued until the names of all the major speaking roles were written up on the two boards outside the main entrance to the Theatre. As can be imagined, as well as excitement for some there was disappointment for others. In discussing the requirement for two performers for each of the major roles, the Director was at pains to point out that there is no such thing as an A team and a B team. The performers are completely interchangeable. Lots are cast to see which of the main performers takes part in the Premiere, and those not chosen for this automatically fulfil their particular roles in the final performance, which for the cast is as momentous as the Premiere itself.

Eva-Maria Reiser and Barbara Dobner will play Mary Magdalene

Carsten Lück and Martin Norz play Judas

CAST LIST FOR 2010

The following are the actors selected to play the most important roles in the 2010 Play.

JESUS
Frederik Mayet	Age 29	Is the Press Officer for the Passion Play. Played John in 2000
Andreas Richter	Age 32	A Psychologist, previously played Archelus, and has been in every Play since 1980

MARY
Ursula Burkhart	Age 28	A professional actress at the Munich Volkstheatre. Has previously played both Mary and Magdalene.
Andrea Hecht	Age 47	Also played Mary in 2000. A housewife.

MARY MAGDALENE
Barbara Dobner	Age 22	A student, she previously appeared in crowd scenes.
Eva-Maria Reiser	Age 24	A Flight attendant, she is also a musician and has previously played in the orchestra for the Play

CAIAPHAS
Anton Burkhart	Age 39	A Forester Was Jesus in 2000
Anton Preisinger	Age 40	A Hotelier Judas in 2000

JUDAS
Carsten Lück	Age 39	He has been building the stage sets in the Passion Play Theatre
Martin Norz	Age 44	A Local Government Officer, he played Jesus in both 1990 and 2000

PETER
Jonas Konsek	Age 22	Student. Has been in previous crowd scenes.
Maximillian Stöger	Age 20	A student, also appeared in previous play crowd Scenes

JOHN
Benedikt Geisenhof	Age 20	Another student who has previously been in crowd scenes.
Martin Schuster	Age 21	This student has been able to defer his military service for a year to enable him to take part.

PILATE
Christian Bierling	Age 44	Is an innkeeper, but is also involved in the Play as a special effects technician.
Stefan Burkhart	Age 41	A shopkeeper. Played Pilate in 1990 and Caiaphas in 2000.

PRACTICAL INFORMATION

Getting there Those travelling independently need to know that Oberammergau lies some 60 miles south of Munich, which has the nearest International Airport, connected with the city centre by a regular fast rail service. Munich is in turn connected with Oberammergau by a regular train service which is supplemented during Passion Play seasons.

By road, take the autobahn system to Munich and then the A95 towards Garmisch-Partenkirchen. From Oberau, the scenic approach to the Ammergau Valley is by the B23 via Ettal.

Seeing the Passion Play As we have seen, the vast majority of tickets for the play are sold as part of a package which also includes either one or two nights'

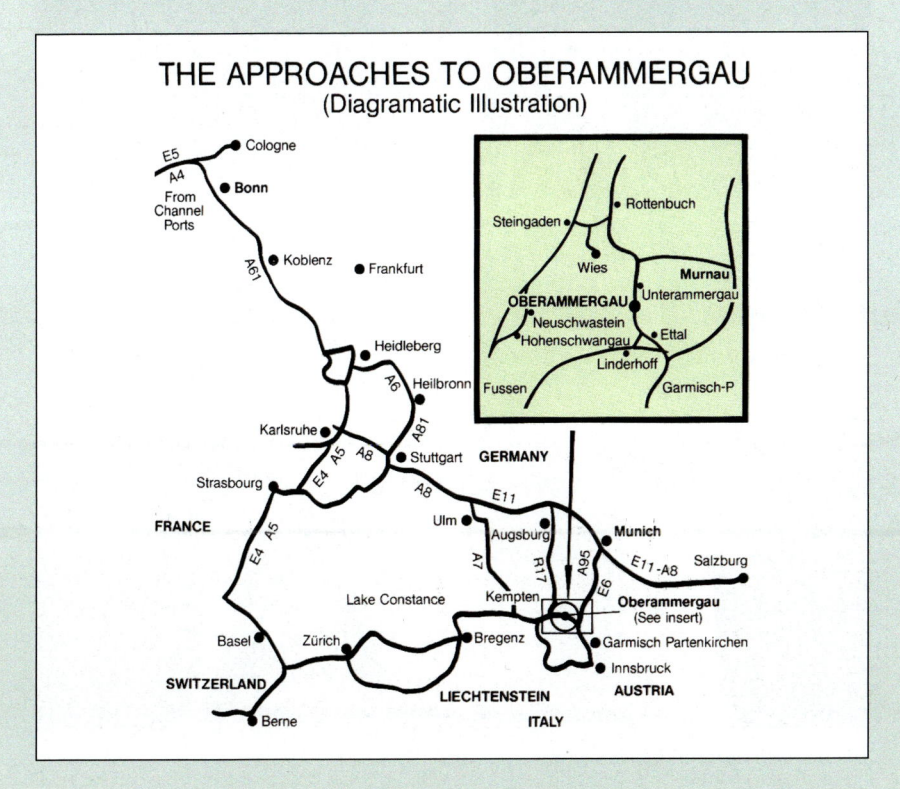

THE APPROACHES TO OBERAMMERGAU
(Diagramatic Illustration)

accommodation and meals. However, some tickets for the Play, without accommodation, are sold to those who either live nearby or can arrange their visit within a single day, and a small number are also sold on the day of performance at a kiosk near the theatre.

All enquiries regarding tickets or other information should be addressed to the Passion Play Office at Eugen-Papst Str. 9a, 82487 Oberammergau. Telephone 08822-9231-0 or Fax 08822-9231-52. The Tourist Office, is at the same address, but on Phone No 08822-922740 (the Code for Germany is 49), and its website is www.oberammergau-passion.com. The e-mail address is info@passionsspiele2010.de

The Kreuzigungsgruppe

A SYNOPSIS OF THE PLAY

This is a brief Synopsis of the Play as it unfolds on stage, which should enable the visitor to follow the action as it happens – it is of course all spoken in German. There is a Text Book which gives a word by word text in English, and this will probably be given to visitors on arrival at the theatre –but it is by no means easy to follow the action on stage and the text in the book at the same time.

Although we have taken into account the changes made up to January 2010, it is still possible that the Directors may change the sequence of some scenes and tableaux.

We think however, that the "plot" is so well known that members of the audience will have no difficulty in following the action.

Prelude – Jesus is proclaimed the Saviour of the World (soloists and chorus)

Tableau – Adam and Eve outside the gate of paradise

Prologue – A Welcome to all brother and sister Pilgrims – united in love for the Saviour

Musical Selection by choir and orchestra

PART ONE OF THE PASSION

Act I – Jerusalem

Jesus enters Jerusalem on a donkey, accompanied by a jubilant crowd.

Tableau – The Israelites – guided by Moses – are saved at the Red Sea

Act II – Jesus with the Friends in Bethany

Prologue – Jesus portrayed as generous healer and miracle worker who is willing to die for those he loves.

Tableau – At the Sinai, the Israelites have to decide: either the golden calf or the God from whom Moses brings down the law.

Bethany – Disciples and friends wonder if Jesus is the promised one. They leave to tell others of the miracles they have witnessed. Jesus asks his disciples "Who do the people think I am?" They respond in various ways – Peter identifies him as the Messiah, the Son of the living God. Jesus calls him "Petros, the Rock" and then challenges all the apostles to proclaim the Kingdom of God

Jesus and his friends, including Lazarus, Magdalene, Martha, Thaddeus, and Andreas are visiting Simon of Cyrene at his home. Judas expects Jesus to be proclaimed King of Israel and liberate them from the Romans. The others agree. Jesus disagrees, but they do not understand.

Magdalene anoints Jesus with a very expensive oil, and Judas objects to the waste of money which could have been better spent on charity. Jesus defends Magdalene and predicts his death at the hands of the Romans. He describes his dying both as defeat and victory. Magdalene and John understand.

Peter suggests Jesus remains in the safety of his home, and Jesus calls him "Satan". When asked to bring peace, Jesus tells them that his mission is to spread division, adding that his disciples must deny him, take up the cross and follow him. Whoever wants to save his life will lose it, but whoever loses his life for Jesus' sake, will gain it.

He then sings a spring song, a traditional psalm, to Magdalene and tells her that they will never again be together on earth. She responds with the passage from the Song of Songs – "Strong as death is love".

Judas and Thomas ask Jesus to make arrangements for their material welfare if he really intends to leave them. Jesus tells them to stop worrying about such mundane matters. Judas insists.

Mary, along with Joseph, Simon, Jacob, Judas, and other relatives of Jesus come on stage. Mary is concerned and others accuse him of irresponsibility because he has not settled down and started a family. Jesus tells them that they will weep and lament, but the world will rejoice. Eventually, sadness will be transformed into joy. He tells his mother that he must be led to slaughter. All leave, except for Judas who says that he is tired of believing and hoping.

Act III – Jesus expels the merchants – Caiphas encounters Pilate – The High Council

Jesus drives the money changers from the Temple. Several merchants protest, Jesus and the crowd start to sing a traditional Jewish pilgrimage psalm, praising God.

Caiaphas, the High Priest (appointed by Pilate), challenges the authority of Jesus to act in the Temple. Jesus answers a question with a question of his own, and refuses to back down to Caiaphas or to answer the original question. Instead he tells the parable of the dishonest, murderous tenants.

Children and crowd shout Hosanna and proclaim Jesus the Messiah (a term which is interpreted as a challenge against Rome). Dariabas and Ezechiel order them to stop. They don't. Jesus presents a child to them as an example. He and his followers leave.

Ezechiel, Nathaniel, and Archelus urge Caiaphas to have Jesus arrested for leading the people astray and undermining the foundation of their faith. Caiaphas counsels patience because Jesus has too many followers and a riot might result.

Tableau – The Paschal Meal before the Exodus from Egypt

Prologue – Describes Jesus aflame with God's spirit, struggling for humankind, and like Moses, gathering around him those who love the Father with their whole being.

In the meantime the choir of the ones who do homage to the golden calf can be heard.

Back in Jerusalem – On the journey, Jesus preaches the Beatitudes. His followers speak of his miracles. Archeus worries that he will cause a popular uprising and Nathaniel accuses Jesus and his followers of having abandoned the God of Israel. Peter and Andreas assure him that they are good Jews. Jesus retaliates by calling them whitewashed tombs, filled with decay.

The crowd shouts Hosanna, and is chased out of the Temple courtyards by a mob.

Tableau – Daniel in the lions' den – model for Passion Play 2010

Caiaphas, Nathaniel, and others discuss ways of stopping Jesus from destroying the very foundation of their form of Judaism, and punishing him for his defiance and arrogance. Nicodemus and Gamaliel object.

NB – there were at the time many differing factions of Judaism whose adherents differed widely in their interpretation of essential issues such as life after death.

Jesus' enemies are afraid to capture him, in public because of his huge following.

Judas enters, and offers to lead them to Jesus. They are suspicious but decide to accept the offer. Judas will be paid 30 pieces of silver, the price of a slave. After Judas leaves, the others, despite the passionate objections of Nicodemus and Joseph of Arimathea, decide that Jesus must die.

Act IV – Jesus celebrates with his disciples the last supper

Tableau – Violence against Job at the rock of Gibeon

Tableau – Moses before the burning bush

Prologue – Jesus and his friends celebrate the night when the Lord freed his people from Egyptian bondage to lead them into the promised land.

Passion Narrative (Soloists and chorus) – Moses' meal filled with hope for the coming of the Lord, prefigures the meal that jesus shared with his friends.

Musical Selection – A chorus of Israelites calls for liberation from Egyptian servitude.

The Last Supper – As is common at a Passover Seder, John, the youngest participant, asks Jesus to tell the story of the Exodus. He does so and goes on to quote Isaiah's dark words of war, violence, and lack of love. He speaks of the Last Judgement and the way the merciful will inherit the kingdom whilst those who have shown no mercy and did not recognise that we love God by loving the unlovable among us will go to eternal punishment.

Jesus then speaks the traditional Passover blessing over the wine. He tells his friends that he came from the Father and is about to go back to the Father, but will return to the world. He then washes their feet and asks them to serve one another as he has served them. Together they pray "Our Father".

After the foot washing he shares bread and wine with his disciples while anticipating and interpreting his death. This scene brings together the motifs of the Passover meal and allusions to the blood of the covenant, the crucifixion, and the heavenly banquet in the Father's kingdom. This moment is remembered by Christians whenever they participate in the Sacrament of Holy Communion.

Judas leaves after Jesus has accused him of planning his betrayal, and Jesus and the others get ready to go to the Mount of Olives.

Act V – **Jesus at the Mount of Olives**

Scene 1 – Judas and his fellow conspirators are approaching. Judas tells them how they will be able to recognise their quarry by his kiss.

Prologue – In despair, Jesus pleads with the Father to save him from the agony to come. But like Moses, he accepts God's will.

Musical Selection – Moses' terror is portrayed as he encounters the burning bush. God's voice calling Moses. His futile struggle against the Lord's command; his excuses, and his ultimate acceptance of the awesome responsibility to lead the People of Israel out of Egypt.

Passion Narrative – Jesus is seen kneeling in the olive grove, weeping and screaming in terror, yet he offers himself to the Father.

Scene 2 – In the olive grove, Jesus and the disciples discuss the events to come. There is much confusion and misunderstanding. Thomas expects Jesus to crush his enemies. Jacob expects the Lord to protect him. John expresses disappointment that Jesus did not save Israel. Andreas reminds Jesus that he and the others have left everything behind to follow him, and wonders what they will receive in exchange. Peter asks where they should go. Jesus insists that he was born for this moment. Yet he fears what is to come. He tells the disciples that they will take offence at him, and that Peter will deny him. He also predicts that they will be persecuted for his sake and be filled with the Spirit of Truth when needed.

Jesus prays alone. The disciples have fallen asleep. Jesus pleads for mercy and yet is ready to accept God's will. He is almost overcome with the weight of humanity's sins.

An Angel appears, and speaks for the Lord, asking Jesus to allow himself to be pierced and crushed by humanity's sins in order that salvation might reach unto the ends of the earth. Jesus accepts the charge.

Judas and the rabble arrive, along with some of the priests. Judas hurries up to Jesus and kisses him. Peter strikes Malchus' ear with his sword, and Jesus heals the wound, after commanding Peter to put his sword away. He then gjves himself up to be arrested.

Musical Selection – The Chorus sings of the coming battle of agony and we are reminded in a duet that the shackles on the hands of Jesus are ransom for our freedom.

PART TWO OF THE PASSION

Tableau – The Prophet Daniel in the lions' den – sentenced to death because he honoured his God. The Chorus sings that in the end, justice will be done, wherever the voice of truth is smothered and the powerful oppress.

Tableau – Job in Misery – taunted by family and friends, bearing the torment patiently.

Act VI – Jesus is brought before Annas and the High Council

Tableau – the despair of Cain who has killed his brother

The Mocking
Peter's Betrayal and Repentance

Prologue – Describes the nocturnal interrogation and compares Jesus to Daniel and Job – mocked, abused, suffering in silence.

Before Annas – Peter and John are discussing the fate of Jesus in the courtyard of Annas' house. What will happen to Jesus? John and Peter exit. Annas and other Council members come on stage. They are anxiously waiting for Jesus to be brought before them. Councillors and temple guards arrive with their prisoner.

Annas interrogates Jesus, asking him what he has been teaching, and accusing him of misleading the people and pretending to be greater than Abraham. Jesus replies that Annas should question his audience, and one of the men slaps him for impudence. Annas accuses him of dissenting from the renowned teachers and denigrating the office of priests. He tells the priests that Jesus must die before the festival.

Act VII – Peter's denial and the despair of Judas

Judas becomes very agitated when he hears that Jesus will die. He hurries off when Annas dismisses his concerns.

Several members of the Temple guard and women are trying to keep warm by a fire, when Jesus is dragged toward them. Peter and John enter and are invited by the men to join them. John and Peter approach the fire. The guards decide to entertain themselves by manhandling and mocking their prisoner, calling him a king of fools and spitting at him.

When Peter is accused of being one of the Nazarene's disciples, he vigorously and repeatedly denies even knowing Jesus, and finally tears himself loose.

Jesus is taken to Caiaphas to be arraigned. Peter deeply regrets his cowardly denial of his friend and teacher and promises that nothing will ever separate him from Jesus again.

Tableau – Moses is expelled by the pharaoh

Prologue – Like Cain, Judas despairs of being worthy of mercy and is driven toward the abyss.

Before Caiaphas – Before members of the High Council enter, Judas considers pleading for his rabbi's life, and returning the blood money.

Jesus is being interrogated by Caiaphas in the presence of other members of the Council. He says nothing in response to Caiaphas' questions. Before the indictment is read, Gamaliel warns the other members of the Council to keep the law and do justice. Jesus is charged with a number of religious violations including blasphemy.

Two witnesses testify to the accuracy of the charges. Jesus does not defend himself.

Gamaliel points out that Jesus is not accused of a crime that is punishable by death or imprisonment.

When asked whether he is the Messiah, Jesus responds in the affirmative.

Gamaliel comes to Jesus' defence, insisting that he considers him a faithful Jew. The others find him guilty of blasphemy, a capital crime. Since only the Romans have the right to order and conduct executions, Jesus will next be taken to the Governor's office.

Judas rushes in and accuses the Council of condemning and murdering an innocent man and pleads for Jesus' life. When he realises that no one listens he curses himself and the members of the Council and plans to commit suicide by hanging himself.

Act VIII – Jesus is brought before Pilate and Herod

Tableau – Joseph is celebrated as saviour and King of Egypt

Prologue – Like the deluded Pharaoh who refused to let God's people go, Pilate refuses to listen to the truth.

Scene 1 – Before Pilate
Members of the Council expect Pilate to support their decision if for no other reason than to gain favour with his appointee, Caiaphas.

Pilate treats the members of the High Council with arrogant disdain, angry at being awakened and their presumption that Caesar's Governor should serve as a blind tool for carrying out their decisions. When told that Jesus called himself the son of God he considers the entire proceeding superstitious nonsense.

Caiaphas then accuses Jesus of being an agitator, a revolutionary.

Pilate admits that he has heard of Jesus, a vagrant, performing magic tricks, but doubts that he is responsible for riots. Caiaphas and the others use Jesus' claim to be the Messiah as proof, since both Jews and Romans understand the term to point to a military leader who will liberate the Jews from the Romans.

Pilate tries to interrogate Jesus who tells him that his kingdom is not of this world. Pilate refuses to authorise the execution, and when he discovers that Jesus comes from Galilee, sends him to Herod, the King of Galilee, who happens to be in Jerusalem for the festival.

Scene 2 – Before Herod
Herod tries to get Jesus to entertain him by causing darkness to fall suddenly or walking without touching the ground, or changing a stick into a snake. When Jesus doesn't perform, he calls him a fool who should be let go. Herod has no intention of getting involved in the pious squabbles of the religious leaders, and after mockingly dressing him in one of his old ceremonial robes, sends Jesus back to Pilate.

Scene 3 – Before Pilate
Caiaphas and Annas do their best to convince Pilate to have Jesus executed. They tell Pilate that they will appeal to the Emperor if Pilate sets Jesus free, and gives him the chance to incite the people to riot, to have him blaspheme the faith, and to have him lead the Jews from under the Roman sword.

Pilate agrees to release either Barabbas or Jesus for the Passover festival. Annas and Caiaphas tell some of the other priests to summon their supporters from the streets and do their best to discourage the followers of Jesus from joining the crowd.

Pilate is told of his wife's request to free Jesus, but is more concerned with potentially using Jesus to keep Barabbas, a real revolutionary, from being set free. He orders Jesus flogged by his men.

Jesus is beaten viciously and collapses. His tormentors dress him in the king's mantle, put the crown of thorns on his head, and hand him a stick for a sceptre. They throw themselves down before Jesus, jeering "We greet you, great and mighty King of the Jews!"

Act IX – Jesus "the King", before the Crowd – Pilate Condemns Jesus to Death

Prologue – In Jesus, the man of sorrows, robbed of all dignity, God's love reveals itself and true majesty is shown. As once Joseph saved the starving nation, Jesus saves humanity

Outrage
Nicodemus tells John that Jesus was condemned to death by the High Council and was then taken before the Governor. Nicodemus still hopes that Pilate won't co-operate. Different groups of people are screaming their support of Barabbas or Jesus. Members of the High Council list the crimes of which Jesus has been

accused and urge their followers to clamour for Barabbas to be pardoned. The mob screams that Jesus should pay for his blasphemy on the cross.

In vain, Nicodemus tries to reason with Caiaphas and the others, who accuse him of being followed by prostitutes and tax collectors, and even pagans.

Finally, as Pilate appears, the frenzied mob demands the death of Jesus. Nicodemus and his followers call for setting Jesus free, but they are outnumbered. When Barabbas is brought in, the mob calls for his liberation. When Pilate continues to hesitate, Caiaphas accuses him of not being Caesar's friend and Annas threatens to inform the Emperor that he gave protection to one guilty of high treason. Among screams of "Crucify Him" Pilate gives in to their demands. He announces that the death sentence will be prepared in writing and proclaimed in public, and Jesus will be crucified with two murderers.

As the sentence is proclaimed, the crosses are brought. Caiaphas and the other priests rejoice over their victory. The people head for Golgotha – the place of skulls.

Act X – The Way of the Cross – The Crucifixion

Prologue – Life, compassion, and grace flow for humanity from the cross

Tableau – Isaac, son of Abraham, carries the wood for his own sacrifice up Mount Moriah

Tableau – Looking at the bronze serpent brings salvation to the Israelites (4 Mos.21.8).

The Way of the Cross
Mary, Lazarus and Magdalene wonder why the streets are deserted. John tries to keep Mary from going to Golgotha, but she insists, recalling Simeon's prophecy when she brought the infant Jesus to the Temple.

To the hate filled scream of the mob, driven with sticks, Jesus staggers up the mountain. He stumbles and falls. The guards drag Jesus along. Mary recognises her son. Veronica wipes his face. One of the soldiers forces Simon of Cyrene to carry the cross. A woman asks, "Rabbi, this is how they reward you?" Jesus asks her to weep for herself and her children.

The Crucifixion
Prologue – On the cross, Jesus asks the Father to forgive his enemies and filled with love, gives up his life, so we will escape eternal death.

When Annas sees the raised cross he is at first delighted, but objects to the inscription "Jesus the Nazarene, King of the Jews". He demands that it be torn down, but is informed that the inscription was attached to the cross by order of the Governor and could not be removed.

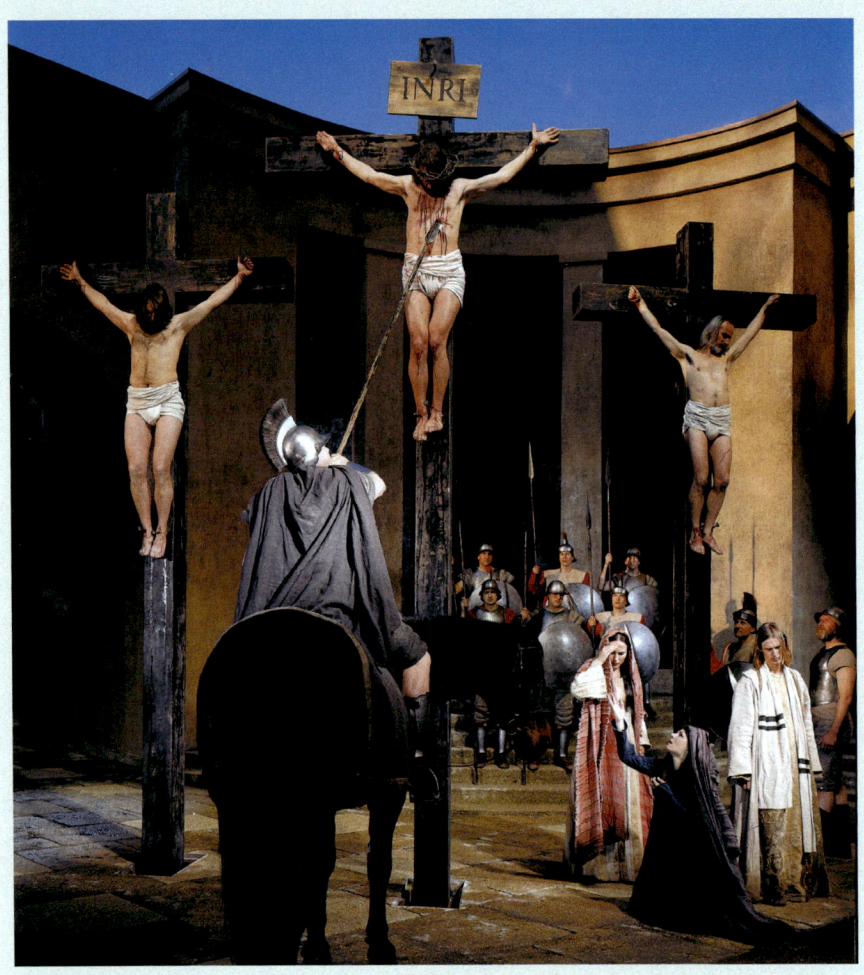

The Crucifixion

    Members of the High Council and some of the Roman soldiers taunt Jesus. The soldiers throw dice for his clothing. After one of the soldiers mocks him, Jesus asks the Father to forgive them, for they don't know what they are doing. His words apply to both Romans and Jews, as well as all of humanity. When one of the robbers asks for mercy from Jesus, he promises that the man will be in paradise that very day. Caiaphas and his followers are appalled at Jesus' arrogance.

    Mary and John are approaching the cross. Jesus asks them to be each other's support. A soldier offers a drink to Jesus. After calling to the Father and commending his spirit to him, Jesus dies.

It begins to thunder. The earth quakes. The sun grows dark. Several spectators ask Almighty God to have mercy on them. The High Priest is told that the curtain of the Holy of Holies in the Temple has torn.

When the friends of Jesus hear that the corpses of the dead are to be thrown into the pit of criminals, Joseph of Arimathea decides to ask Pilate for the body of Jesus, so he can be buried in an appropriate tomb. Nicodemus offers to bring the oils to embalm him.

Mary and Magdalene plead with the soldiers to spare Jesus when they break the bones of the others. After Jesus' side has been pierced with a lance, and they are sure he is dead, the soldiers consent.

Members of the High Council are concerned that the disciples of Jesus could steal the body and then spread the story that he had risen again, as he had prophesied.

John, Magdalene, and Mary are mourning, Magdalene reminds them of the words Jesus said when he departed from Bethany. "You will weep and lament, but the world will rejoice. You will be sad, but your sadness will be transformed into joy. And no one will be able to take away your joy."

Mary comforts Jesus

After Nicodemus and the other men have taken Jesus down from the cross they place his body on Mary's lap. She speaks of him as "The light that came into the world, so that no one who believes in Him might ever perish".

Act XI – The Resurrection

Prologue – Jesus Lives. The annointed one arises and leads humanity toward the heavenly source of all life.

Appearance of the Risen Jesus

The Roman soldiers are tired of keeping watch at the tomb. The women enter on their way to the tomb. Magdalene says how happy she is to be able to pay final honours to her beloved Rabbi. They worry about the heavy stone. Then they notice that the stone has been moved and the tombs is empty. Magdalene enters the tomb where an Angel tells her not to worry, that Jesus has arisen from the dead.

Outside, Jesus speaks to her, but she doesn't recognise him at first. When she does, he asks her to tell the others what has happened. Magadelene rejoices – "I Have seen the Lord, I have heard His voice! I know that my saviour lives …. Oh, could I proclaim it throughout all the world, that the mountains and rocks and heaven and earth should re-echo with the words

HALLELUJA! HE IS RISEN!

Concluding meditation – musical selection. The chorus sings a hymn of praise and jublilation.